Taxing Illusions
Taxation, Democracy and
Embedded Political Theory

Phillip Hansen

Fernwood Publishing • Halifax

Copyright © 2003 Phillip Hansen

All rights reserved. No part of this book may be reproduced or transmitted in any form or by any means without permission in writing from the publisher, except by a reviewer, who may quote brief passages in a review.

Editing: Brenda Conroy
Design and production: Beverley Rach
Printed and bound in Canada by: Hignell Printing Limited

A publication of:
Fernwood Publishing
Site 2A, Box 5, 8422 St. Margaret's Bay Road
Black Point, Nova Scotia, B0J 1B0
and 324 Clare Avenue
Winnipeg, Manitoba, R3L 1S3
www.fernwoodbooks.ca

Fernwood Publishing Company Limited gratefully acknowledges the financial support of the Department of Canadian Heritage, the Nova Scotia Department of Tourism and Culture and the Canada Council for the Arts for our publishing program.

National Library of Canada Cataloguing in Publication

Hansen, Phillip
Taxing illusions: taxation, democracy and embedded political theory / Phillip Hansen.

(Fernwood basics)
Includes bibliographical references.
ISBN 1-55266-102-4

1. Fiscal policy—Canada. 2. Taxation—Political aspects—Canada.
I. Title. II. Series.

HJ2460.S3H35 2003   339.5'25'0971   C2003-900129-6

Contents

Acknowledgements 5
Preface 7

1. Taxation, Democracy and Political Theory 10

2. Taxation as an Expression of Community:
   Report of the Saskatchewan Royal Commission
   on Taxation (1965) 24

3. Taxation as a Barrier to Wellbeing:
   Final Report of the Saskatchewan Personal Income
   Tax Review Committee (1999) 45

4. Taxation, the Role of the State and
   the Dynamics of Political Culture 71

5. A Tale of Two Studies: "Embedded Political Theory"
   and Democracy 88

6. The "Free" Market, Embedded
   Political Theory—and Us 113

Bibliography *121*

for Michael

Acknowledgements

The idea for this study was first suggested to me in 1999 in an email from Larry Haiven, then at the University of Saskatchewan, now at St. Mary's University in Halifax. Larry drew attention to the report of the 1965 Saskatchewan Royal Commission on Taxation and indicated how its position differed dramatically from currently dominant thinking on questions about taxation, especially as reflected in the then recently completed report of the Saskatchewan Personal Income Tax Review Committee. The initial version of the argument was developed in a (overly long) paper presented at the 2001 Annual Meeting of the Atlantic Provinces Political Studies Association at the University of New Brunswick-Saint John. The kindness and support extended to me by the wonderful people responsible for this excellent academic forum made it easier to present the ideas explored here, ideas of whose justification I was anything but certain. I am particularly grateful to Joanna Everitt, who invited me to participate in the conference, and to Thom Workman, who as my discussant offered sympathy and encouragement. (And Thom's excellent book, *Banking on Deception: The Discourse of Fiscal Crisis*, served as a model for my own.) Wayne Antony of Fernwood Publishing suggested I expand the paper into a book and also has offered his usual combination of sound editorial advice and enthusiastic support. Bob Ware of the University of Calgary and an anonymous Fernwood reader provided many insightful criticisms that encouraged me to clarify more fully my arguments and ideas; the book is stronger for their efforts. Dave Gullickson, Joyce Green, Karen Murray, Paul Barber, Michael Rushton and Ken Rasmussen graciously read earlier versions of these ideas and gave helpful suggestions and comments. Paul Browne did likewise and through his own work also reminded me of the importance of the concept of "reification." Alvin Finkel brought to the manuscript his finely honed sense of the necessary connection between history and philosophy and offered helpful suggestions about the historical context in which questions raised in the book have emerged. My conversations with Gary Tompkins helped me clarify my understanding of concepts in economics (he is not of course responsible for the use I have made of these). The Bushwakker seminar participants—Joe Roberts, Sheila Roberts, Lorne Brown and Fay Hutchinson—willingly provided a forum for the generation and development of these ideas and otherwise sustained me with the warmth and good humour that are the hallmarks of deep and abiding friendship.

When all was said and done, Brenda Conroy did an expert job in copyediting the manuscript. Thank you also to Beverley Rach for the book design and Barbara Parker for proofreading and inputting.

Laureen Gatin provides unstinting encouragement and support in so many ways. I am grateful to her far beyond anything I can say.

My son, Michael Joel-Hansen, is a constant source of pride and delight. His generation will bear the consequences of political decisions made now. I dedicate this book to him.

Preface

This book had its origins in a hunch and an assumption. The hunch was that a comparison of two, admittedly obscure, studies of the tax system in the province of Saskatchewan, one undertaken in the early 1960s, the other in the late 1990s, would reflect the significant shift, over the last three decades, in the ideological climate and the foundations of public policy in Western liberal democratic capitalist states, including Canada. Much has been written about the transformation of Keynesian or social democratic political and economic values to neo-liberal views about the need to "free" markets and correspondingly reduce the role of the state in the economy. I believe that the detailed discussion of these studies, which forms the heart of this work, offers particularly compelling evidence of this shift.

The assumption is more difficult to explain and more controversial. It is that in a culture as resolutely individualist as our own—and in many respects significantly more so now than it has been for decades—it is nonetheless impossible to think coherently about who we are as individuals, and what politics is or should be about, without at the same time thinking about community as more than simply an aggregation of individuals whose self-seeking behaviour requires co-ordination. The question of community is inherently a normative one: we unavoidably confront the issue of what does and should bind us together collectively.

Because of the critical role taxation plays in the modern state and because the state is central to the ties that bind, tax studies like the two considered here necessarily offer observations, claims and judgments which evoke images and understandings about our lives together. Concerns about community, the nature of individuals and the dimensions of social life stand at the core of political theory or philosophy. In this light, the studies examined in this book provide evidence of what I call *embedded political theory*: judgments about the appropriate character of human social bonds, about how we should live together. Such judgements set out necessary and possible forms of purposes and actions, both individual and collective. I suggest that the real and enduring significance of the two studies, and by extension all documents of this sort, lies here, at the level of fundamental and largely unstated commitments and that in unearthing and examining these commitments we unavoidably confront our own.

The judgments and commitments entailed by the idea of embedded political theory are also in the world at large, in the institutions and practices, the organized forms of human activity, that constitute society. Indeed, policy documents "make sense" because they refer to social forms that also "make sense." In other words, such documents hold embedded assumptions about human goals and purposes. In this book, I use the term "embedded" to refer to ideas that inform both policy studies and social institutions.

Coming to terms with our own commitments in the face of embedded ideas is not a neutral process of identification and characterization. We are, potentially at least, changed by this encounter in that we recognize certain things about our selves and our society that impinge upon our wants, needs and purposes, that is, what we are ultimately about as individuals and as members of a body politic. We may come to recognize that certain ways of defining our situation stand at odds with deeply entrenched dimensions of individual and social expectations and experiences. I believe that neo-liberalism, which has become so dominant in recent years, conflicts with fundamental commitments relating to self and society and therefore offers an unsustainable basis for both individual identity and political institutions.

Embedded political theory provides an account of the inescapable normative dimensions of political language and policy analysis and, at the same time, an encounter with our own unavoidable assumptions, values and commitments—and both dimensions are necessarily intertwined. The idea that an account of the embedded value-laden assumptions of policy documents is itself value-laden informs the approach taken in this book. This is particularly apparent in two elements of this study. The first is the argument that any policy study, while appearing to be merely descriptive or analytical, is necessarily normative, or value laden, and we cannot avoid confronting this if we want to fully understand it. The second involves the articulation of my own commitments and judgments about the issues discussed.

Ultimately, the idea of embedded political theory is rooted in the claim that political authority and public policy are not just "out there," but "in here." They shape our identities and social practices by informing our sense of what is or is not imaginable, what is or is not possible, what is or is not desirable. The notion of embedded political theory may help bring policy questions and policy analysis alive, for students of policy to be sure, but also for citizens, who, ideally, must decide what is to be done to address public concerns. The role and nature of democracy—what kinds of social and political values, practices and institutions are involved in achieving it—are very much at issue. My sense is that the idea of embedded political theory might prove useful in illuminating questions of democratic theory and practice.

Hence the title of this book: the idea of "taxing illusions" has a double meaning. Claims about taxation and appropriate tax policy can be illusory. They can mislead about the political, economic and social significance of taxation itself. The frequently expressed view that taxation involves forcibly taking from people what is rightfully theirs and improperly disposing of it is an illusion of this kind. Illusions such as this can take a toll on our capacity to understand ourselves and our society, at the cost of insight into important questions about how we should live together. In other words, they can "tax," or stress, us because they block our coming to terms with dimensions and dilemmas in our social lives that we need to face. They are taxing *illusions* and *taxing* illusions.

This work thus is a study in political language and its place in shaping conceptions and practices of self and the world. Words and expressions do not just represent our world but also help construct it. Language and action are closely intertwined. Our capacity for both, our nature as it were, makes possible the kinds of experiences we identify as distinctively human. What we think, say and do are necessarily connected. This is especially important to understand in relation to politics, where the empirical and the normative—facts and values—intersect and shape how we confront issues of human living together.[1]

This study tries to grasp the complexities of social experience, including the nature of democracy, in the contemporary era, when neo-liberal views and policies have come to prominence. In this respect, it seeks to explore the world of political and intellectual culture, the realm of ideas and their role in shaping the kind of society we have. While researching and writing this book, I was reminded how important it is to think carefully about issues of self and society. I hope this work encourages all of us to do so.

Note

1. For excellent treatments of these questions from the perspectives of, respectively, political theory and political sociology, see Hanna Fenichel Pitkin, *Wittgenstein and Justice* (1972) (Berkeley: University of California Press, 1993); and the extensive work of Murray Edelman, notably *Political Language: Words That Succeed and Policies That Fail* (New York: Academic Press, 1977) and *The Politics of Misinformation* (Cambridge: Cambridge University Press, 2001).

Chapter One

Taxation, Democracy and Political Theory

This book is a case study in the use of the tools of political theory for the conduct of policy analysis. It examines two policy documents prepared for the government of Saskatchewan, at two different points of time, in order to illustrate changing conceptions of appropriate public policy and the proper role of the state in contemporary society. Both reports analyze and make recommendations about a fundamental issue confronting governments everywhere: taxation.

No doubt, most people know the old cliché: "There are only two things in life that are certain: death and taxes." Few would deny that taxation stands at the heart of the modern state, that indeed it is a "tax state."[1] No other dimension or function of the state seems as visible or prone to conflict and controversy. Less obviously, however, taxation represents a core bond, tying individuals together. In modern societies, the state is central to forging that systemic and enduring pattern of interactions we know as "the political community." It provides a crucial and ordered means of bringing together people whose paths and purposes intersect in multiple and complex ways. It articulates in a fundamental sense the ties of the community. In the measure that taxation defines the modern state, the values, institutions, practices and policies associated with taxation invariably shape the meaning of citizenship. They not only flesh out our rights and obligations but also our conceptions of what count as worthwhile, appropriate and possible commitments and actions. Joseph Schumpeter, an important early-twentieth-century economist, saw the tax state as the way in which a modern capitalist society addresses its common material wants and needs. But he also believed it represented much more than that:

> If the tax state were to fail and another form of providing for the wants of the community ensued, this would ... mean much more than that a new fiscal system replaces the [previous] one. Rather, what we call the modern state would itself change its nature; the economy would have to be driven by new motors along new paths; the social structure could not remain what it is; the approach to life and its cultural contents, the spiritual outlook of individuals—everything would have to change.[2]

Of course, any examination of taxation must evidently be sensitive to tax policies as such, to the professed principles and goals of such policies and to the constellation of interests shaping and determining them. But it must also be attuned to the ways in which such policies and purposes illuminate the character of our social and political bonds and our political identities. In examining tax policies, we need to look at more than how governments raise and spend revenue or even how different groups in society both seek to influence tax policy and are affected by it. The taxation system and changes to it tell us about the character of public life in society at a particular point in time. They provide clues about widely held political values and possibilities and whether and how these become legitimate, or normatively binding on people. They also give insight into the forces fashioning the contours of state, economy and society and the characteristics of political, social and economic institutions. The struggle to define, expand or limit the power to tax is an ongoing part of the process that determines how politics and political institutions shape society and the roles individuals and groups play within it.

While a tax regime, a set of tax policies, practices and institutions, typically emerges from the "normal," everyday play of political forces, at certain points in time the tax regime itself may become a specific object of attention. This happens either because there is the perceived need to consolidate an existing set of understandings or practices, or because the current arrangements are under challenge. In the latter circumstance, the roles of politics and institutions are likely to be called into question. They will no longer hold in the face of social change. Social forces may press for alternatives to arrangements they no longer accept (or in some cases may never accepted).

Tax reform may thus become an explicit policy initiative. In pressing this initiative, governments typically resort to one of more of an array of policy instruments, notably commissions or committees of investigation. These provide an opportunity for social interests to make their cases on behalf of their preferred policy choices. But they also serve as a mechanism for articulating the assumptions and commitments underlying the perceptions people have of what is at stake and what is to be done about it.

The role of taxation and the ways in which tax policy enters into and shapes the political agenda of the contemporary state raise two sets of issues or questions. One involves the matter of *who* determines policy and *how* this is done. The other relates to the *terms* under which political claims, policy analysis, public debate and state commitments are carried out. Put otherwise, the first set of concerns raises the question of *democracy*. It is about power in the state and who controls it. Asking who determines policy raises the matter of access to the institutions of political decisionmaking. Democracy is concerned with both the extent and kind of such access. For example, as discussed below, whether access involves selecting people to act on one's behalf or actual hands-on engagement in making decisions is a fundamental question that has for over a century molded political values in liberal democratic societies.

The second set of concerns raises the matter of *public discourse* or (using the term loosely and generally) *ideology*. It involves the role of language in shaping society and individual identities. Before turning to the discussion of taxation, I touch on each set of concerns, since both are central to my analysis.

One claim of this study is that democracy and public discourse are closely connected. Obviously, what people do, or believe possible and desirable to do, has always been closely tied to what they think, say and write about who they are and how the world is structured. But it could be argued that in the contemporary era, characterized by increasingly sophisticated and pervasive forms of mass communications, the tie between democracy and discourse is both tighter and more taken for granted. Our world is full of political symbols, claims, concepts and catchwords that are widely available and used to describe situations and to offer explanations and judgments. The sheer volume of "talk," some meaningful and insightful, much not, testifies to the capacity of our society to make a culture of ideas, good and bad, ever more extensive and even inescapable. It is no coincidence that important currents of contemporary social analysis emphasize the question of "voice"—whether, where and how a person can speak to their own needs. We live in what the American social theorist and media analyst, Todd Gitlin, has called a "society saturated by mass media,"[3] a media-dominated public sphere, where the demand for ideas and images and the ability to both fabricate and disseminate them widely and rapidly have grown dramatically. Even academic ideas, which have become central to tax policies and debates, have entered the mix, as universities have come to assume a highly visible public role.

Especially in societies that are politically democratic, power has always involved elements of symbolism and legitimacy, of credibility and persuasion. Public opinion cannot be managed autocratically and dictatorially, at least not directly or most of the time.[4] *Who* has a say is closely tied to *what* is said, *where* it is said and *how* it is said. None of these is forever fixed; all are subject to change over time as social and political forces strive to influence the agenda of political deliberation and decisionmaking. Changes in the content and context of tax policy have reflected this, as I show later on.

Propaganda is one means by which powerful interests seek to persuade citizens of a democracy to pursue courses of action favourable to their purposes (and to dissuade them from pursuing others).[5] But what interests me here is the fact that certain ideas come, in a seemingly organic way, to assume credibility, to take on the character of an almost unquestioned common sense—that is, widely held, everyday understandings of themselves and their society that people acquire through their participation in social life. The strength of such common sense "arises from its consonance with a range of intersubjective ideas, narratives or themes embedded within popular consciousness."[6] Credible ideas do not have to be widely embraced explicitly; it is enough that notions which might contest them are seen as beyond the pale, as unrealistic, ultimately as failing to "make sense." For example, Thom Workman notes that there is a powerful tendency in everyday political language to equate a government's financial situation with that of an individual, business or family; this has been critical for the emergence of the idea that Canada has been facing a deficit and debt crisis (more on this below).[7] The two situations are not equivalent: the government is not only backed by the enormous wealth of the public sector and has access to revenues through bonds and taxation no individual of family possesses, but through its laws creates the conditions for the generation of private wealth itself. But this idea is very difficult to present to people in an understandable way, which is not only or even primarily a question of any inherent difficulty in grasping the idea. It is also a matter of the powerful support given the analogy between public and personal finances by the organs of public opinion, be these the media, business, policy think-tanks or political figures. For most people, it just makes sense that if individuals or families can spend too much and face bankruptcy, so too can governments. People don't necessarily therefore conclude that there is a crisis of government indebtedness requiring radical measures such as dramatic cuts to government spending. In fact, even in the mid-1990s, when the emphasis on deficit and debt reduction was at its peak, a substantial number of people supported maintaining spending on government social and healthcare programs at then current levels.[8] But they haven't strongly resisted such spending cuts either. Even if the policies are not universally, or in some cases even widely, accepted, the claims used to justify them are—they are "common sense."

Such dominant ideas do not have to be propagandistic; after all, propaganda always runs the risk of being seen through. In any case, propaganda carries with it the idea of conscious intent to influence, manipulate and deceive. The ideas I explore here in the context of tax policy are for the most part held in good faith by their proponents.[9] Indeed, if they were not, they would be *less* influential and also less open to critical analysis. Ideas that open up for us questions of how we should live are more engaging than those we simply write off as more or less conscious and self-serving rationalizations of someone's interests.[10]

Put another way, if, as I argue, there is at least potentially a tension between their aspirations and their purposes in the everyday consciousness of people, *including those who benefit from the existing relations and institutions of power and authority*, there must be a difference between what concepts mean and how they are used. What I call embedded political theory is based on the claim that political ideas have meaning in and of themselves, a content independent of, although related to, how or by whom they are, or might be, used. Of course, who uses them, and why and how they are used, can help us get a fuller sense of the contexts and purposes shaping the meaning of such ideas. Nonetheless, their meanings cannot be restricted to the contexts of their use, nor can they be reduced to the conscious purposes for which they might be deployed in political debate or discussion. They possess a content reflecting the overall structure of a society and the quest by individuals to achieve a meaningful and fulfilling way of life. In this, in part, lies their "embeddedness." [11]

It is fundamental to the argument of this book that ideas be treated in a sense for their own sake, all the better to appreciate their social content, this "embeddedness." This might seem peculiar, or even perverse: how can we possibly understand the social content of ideas by treating them on their own terms, without apparent direct reference to society, by which is meant, approximately, the social groups using them? But just as we can sometimes understand where we are in geographical space by drawing back from our particular place and getting a picture of the whole scene (or, more metaphorically, get a sense of where we are in social space by withdrawing from that and seeing it in the context of the entire society), so too, we can grasp more clearly the nature of our ideas by a comparable process of "standing back." Things that might not be apparent on first glance can become more visible in this way. In short, rational reflection, which is the core purpose of political theory or philosophy, requires not only relating ideas to social groups but also examining their structure and content. It is part of how, as (potentially) rational beings, we come to assess the rationality of the world, that is, how our lives link up with our fundamental purposes. My hope is that by proceeding in this fashion, the meaning and significance of some of our most important values and practices can become clearer.

Of course, in another sense, ideas do not stand alone. They *are* intertwined with norms, practices and institutions linking individual identities with social life. This study after all is concerned with tax *policies* implemented by *states* embedded in and shaping social and economic *relations*. In the contemporary world, certainly in an advanced capitalist society such as Canada, the point at which ideas, and norms, practices and institutions intersect is democracy.

"Democracy"— which refers to a political system based on political equality and popular rule—has always been a contested concept, open to varying definitions and interpretations. I do not explore these in any great detail here, but I note certain themes which seem relevant to any consideration of how tax policy illuminates important questions of citizenship and community.

For most people, democracy is liberal or representative democracy: the world of voting and elections. It is, in the words of the Canadian political theorist, C.B. Macpherson, "merely a mechanism for choosing and authorizing governments"[12] a system based on "one person, one vote," with individual voters, operating in a competitive system of political parties, selecting those who are to exercise power and make decisions on their behalf and who are ultimately accountable for their deeds. What is represented is the will of the people, formed by equal citizens making their choices at the ballot box.

From time to time however (and we seem now to be in one of those times), representative democracy comes to be viewed as inadequate, flawed, even corrupt. It is no longer seen as expressing the popular will. One key measure of this currently is the sharp decline in voter turnout at elections. This has become especially noteworthy of late in Canada, both federally and provincially. For example, in Canadian federal elections, turnout has declined from previous levels of about 75 percent to just over 62 percent in the 2000 general election. In Saskatchewan, which by Canadian standards has typically enjoyed high turnouts, the level in provincial elections has fallen just as sharply, from over 82 percent in 1991 to approximately 65 percent in 1999.[13]

For Macpherson, periodic dissatisfaction with representative democracy was understandable because alongside it has stood another conception of what democracy is about. In this second view, democracy is not simply about choosing and authorizing governments but rather refers to "a kind of society—a whole complex of relations between individuals—rather than simply a system of government." It is based on the idea that democracy is a form of life facilitating the "equal effective right of individuals to live as fully as they may wish ... to make the most of [themselves]" in all areas of life and not just in the formal political arena.[14] Macpherson felt that this latter form of democracy was more authentic and truer to the spirit of both liberalism and democracy, because it more accurately reflected what he saw as our nature as social beings. He thought that we were not just isolated individuals standing on our own but people who needed and wanted community with others because this was vital to our fulfillment as individuals.[15] As will be shown, this issue is significant in exploring the place of taxation in the contemporary state.

But this claim is a critical judgment about how people live in a liberal democratic capitalist society not an unshakeable truth. (Although when Macpherson made this claim, he believed that pressures for a more democratic society were building.) It does not follow that a crisis of representative democracy will necessarily produce a more fully and richly democratic social order. As history has demonstrated, it can result in an avowedly authoritarian and even despotic political system. For example, it is not obvious that the current disaffection with representative democracy in Canada is being fuelled by a desire for a richer kind of democracy, in Macpherson's sense of the term, or will lead to one.

Nonetheless, the distinction Macpherson draws is helpful because it raises the question of citizenship, membership in the political community, and what this involves. Specifically, it suggests there are two ways in which people can relate to the political order. If democratic citizenship is strictly about choosing and authorizing governments, then the political community as represented by the state stands in some sense apart from individuals who, through voting, seek to bring their interests to bear on what the state does. Individuals are, to use the currently fashionable term, "stakeholders." While the state may be necessary, it is also in a manner of speaking disconnected from much that matters to individuals in their lives. Our "real" purposes rest elsewhere. On the other hand, if democratic citizenship involves sustaining a fulfilling set of social relations which permit all equally to make the most of themselves, then the political order or the state is not *apart from*, but rather *a part of*, a life lived in a community that is an integral component of individual fulfillment. Both of these ways of relating to the political order have significant implications for taxation and how people come to view its purposes and "burdens."

Put otherwise, the question of the nature and extent of democracy in modern society raises the question of the nature and extent of politics: What should be the realm of collective decisionmaking by all in the interests of all, in both the state and in society more generally. In this light, an Australian political theorist, John Dryzek, has usefully identified three criteria for defining democracy and its extent, and thus the range of politics: franchise ("the number of participants in any political setting"); scope ("the domains of life under democratic control"); and authenticity ("the degree to which democratic control is substantive rather than symbolic, informed rather than ignorant, and competently engaged").[16] By its nature, taxation addresses all of these.

The role of the state and the place of taxation shape and are shaped by the range of norms, issues and practices that these criteria help illuminate. For individual citizens, the issue of what politics means and what kind of democracy is desirable turns on a fundamental question that in different ways we are all called upon to pose and answer: To what extent can my purposes be fulfilled only together with others; indeed to what extent are my purposes *our* purposes, defined by being shared, and not just mine, alone? With respect to taxation, this raises the question of whether taxes are charges imposed on us by remote political authorities we are always reluctant to pay and do so only because we are coerced, or whether they are self-imposed levies, expressions of our commitment to the wellbeing of all. The answers to these questions are central to assessing policy claims around taxation.

I examine political discourse and democracy more fully later in the book. The remarks here are intended to provide a context for my approach to deliberations about tax policy and in particular shifts in the focus, tenor and logic of policy analysis. For while taxes may be as predictable, unavoidable and permanent as death, tax policy and the assumptions underlying it most assuredly are not.

In Canada in recent years, we have witnessed a spate of tax studies and a vocal emphasis on tax reform.[17] The governments of Alberta, Manitoba, Saskatchewan and Newfoundland established formal tax review bodies. But even without the specific impetus provided by formal studies, both the federal government and other provinces, notably Ontario, have pursued extensive changes to their tax systems.[18]

Contemporary tax reform in Canada has overwhelmingly stressed the need for tax reductions, in particular cuts to taxes on personal and corporate income. Federal and provincial tax policies have followed suit. Tax reductions are held to be necessary in the face of globalization, technological change and the consequent pressures for economic competitiveness. There has been a dramatic increase over the last two decades in the ability of investors to move capital freely around the globe and of companies to establish production facilities in many different locations. This has been complemented by a rapid reduction under liberalized or free trade agreements, of tariff and trade barriers to the flow of goods and services. It is claimed that if Canada is to prosper, it must be able to compete in this new world of freer markets by successfully attracting and retaining mobile capital investment and by ensuring that the costs of producing goods and services for export are kept in line with those of competitor economies.

The pursuit of tax reform in Canada has been part of an international move to reduce taxes on high-income earners and wealth owners, ostensibly to meet the demands of the new "competitiveness." This move among developed countries was spearheaded in the nineteen eighties by the United States and Great Britain and carried to poorer nations by pressures from international organizations such as the World Bank and the International Monetary Fund. Its roots are in the emergence of neo-liberalism, the view that in the interests of both economic prosperity and economic freedom, government intervention into the economy should be reduced and limited and the role of the private market enhanced.[19] In these circumstances, tax reform is a means of elevating market forces over the power of political institutions to pursue goals which might limit these forces.

There was an earlier wave of tax study initiatives. It came in the nineteen sixties, as the post-war welfare state in Canada and elsewhere was being consolidated and the use of state power to manage the capitalist economy in the interests of continuing, stable economic growth and full employment was at its peak.[20] It was a very different world. The ideas of the English economist, John Maynard Keynes, which justified a positive role for the state in the economy, had considerable influence in all advanced capitalist countries. The tax studies of that era in Canada, in particular the study authored by the famous federally appointed Royal Commission on Taxation (the Carter Commission),[21] reflected and supported these ideas.

If I am right about the relation sketched out above between political discourse and democracy, then we can learn much by comparing then with now. The tax studies of each era offer insight into the nature and function of political language: how problems and issues are defined and how people view themselves, or are encouraged to view themselves, as agents and actors. They also tell us about democracy: about government and citizenship, the market and society, the individual and the community. In the final analysis, they put into focus the always tension-laden relation between democracy and capitalism, and what happens if and when the balance between the two shifts.

This book examines two such studies, both undertaken by the government of Saskatchewan: the *Report of the Royal Commission on Taxation* (1965) (the McLeod Report); and the *Final Report and Recommendations of the Saskatchewan Personal Income Tax Committee* (1999) (the Vicq Report). Both indicate how the political landscape of the province has changed from the sixties to today. But their significance is more general than in simply offering interesting insights into the political history of a small province, even one with, by Canadian standards, a distinctive populist and social democratic heritage. They provide case evidence of what the shift from the Keynesian to the neo-liberal era has meant. They indicate what is at stake in debates about taxes: in the contemporary period, the options and choices the currently dominant neo-liberal framework of thought and action establishes. In other words, these studies help us appreciate what it means to live in a neo-liberal world, *to live as if the values of neo-liberalism were 'true.'*

The choice of these two studies also reflects something else. When one discusses political ideas and policy initiatives undertaken by governments and the use of various instruments such as royal commissions or review committees, one faces the question of whose ideas and whose initiatives are being explored. In other words, are the ideas informing the process "widely held" and "legitimate," to use the terms I suggested above, or simply the dominant ideas held by those with the power to present and enforce them? Are policy instruments such as royal commissions "objective" tools or exercises in "legitimation" or public relations, vehicles for a government to rationalize a course of action it has already decided upon behind closed doors?

If I am right in my brief accounts above of both the nature of ideas and the role of taxation, then things are rarely so straightforward. Thus, if my distinction between propaganda and ideology holds up, dominant political ideas held and made effective by the most powerful interests in the society can be, and likely will be, more widely shared and legitimate. Even those disadvantaged by the operation of social institutions which these ideas shape are likely to believe them (as I suggested in my earlier discussion of common sense views about government finance). And whatever the motives of governments in setting up commissions of inquiry to deal with policy questions—sometimes they do so simply because they are uncertain how to proceed—there is always the possibility such commissions will produce surprising and even unwelcome results, if not for governments, then certainly for important social interests.[22] Even a government that intends to serve powerful private interests by its actions might, by adopting an "objective" approach to policymaking, find itself hoisted on its own petard. In any case, the language of such policy devices has, as part of a society, its own structures, practices and history, its own autonomy. Unlike in the world of *Alice in Wonderland*, it cannot just be used as people please. This is why I believe the tax studies examined here can provide insight into important questions about who we are and the kind of social order we might want or need. The studies are, if you like, social artifacts that carry meaning and can be interpreted, "decoded." They are examples of embedded political theory.

In what follows, Chapters Two and Three examine in detail the two Saskatchewan tax studies in order to explore their fundamental assumptions, some explicit, some implicit, about taxes, government and ultimately the nature of individual and social wellbeing. Chapter Four discusses what the differences between the two studies can tell us about the nature of political values, institutions and possibilities. Chapter Five follows this up with an account of a critical approach to political analysis that attempts to offer theoretical and practical insight. This approach involves what I call "embedded political theory," and I identify its primary elements. In the end, I hope to demonstrate how taxation provides a particularly appropriate picture of democratic norms and democracy itself, in the current era in which capitalist values have been ascendant.

Tax studies of the kind examined here are particularly worthy objects of critical scrutiny because they open up three levels of both political analysis and social experience. One level concerns the specific elements of public policy *per se*; this is the manifest or surface content of such studies. A second level involves policy paradigms and ideological frameworks, such as neo-liberalism and Keynesianism. Less overtly visible than that of specific policy arguments, this level can nonetheless become an object of attention, especially when or if there is a paradigm shift. Finally, there is the level of entrenched value commitments and assumptions about human nature and society. This is encased in the language and structure of such reports, what they say or do not say, what they include or leave out. The development of the idea of embedded political theory is an attempt to explore this level.

This book emphasizes political theory because of what it tells us about ourselves. We are all political theorists. We cannot avoid making judgments about, and coming to terms with, who we are as human agents—that is, individuals with distinctive purposes, needs and aspirations—and how we live, and ought to live, with others. And whether we are self consciously aware of it or not—and most of the time we are not—in our day-to-day lives we often think like political theorists. In our self-reflections about what we do and in our attempts to make sense of what others do, we seek not so much to register facts as to discern meaning and exercise judgment. Much of our everyday language is value-laden and normative, the stuff of political theory.

Taxation is a particularly important example of an issue replete with this sort of normative content because it opens up, in such a striking manner, everyday questions about political life. For example, the extent to which we view taxes as burdensome and resent the need to pay them may tell us about how we understand ourselves—as either bound together with others or as on our own—and about how we view society—as either a community from which we all draw material, cultural and moral support and are therefore obligated to nurture because we are inescapably part of it, and it of us, or as an aggregation of otherwise self-contained individuals.

In the final chapter to the book, I explore these themes in a way that I hope will illuminate the core claim of this book: that public policy does not just happen *to* us, it happens *through* us.

Notes

1. See the classic study by Joseph Schumpeter, "The Crisis of the Tax State" (1918), in Richard Swedberg ed., *Joseph A. Schumpeter: The Economics and Sociology of Capitalism* (Princeton: Princeton University Press, 1991), 99–140.
2. Ibid., 100. Schumpeter goes on to argue: "Taxes not only helped create the state. They helped to form it. The tax system was the organ the development of which entailed the other organs. Tax bill in hand, the state penetrated the private economies and won increasing dominion over them. The tax brings money and calculating spirit into corners in which they do not dwell as yet, and thus becomes a formative factor in the very organism which has developed it. The kind and level of taxes are determined by the social structure, but once taxes exist they become a handle, as it were, which social powers can grip in order to change this structure." (108)
3. Todd Gitlin, *The Whole World's Watching: Mass Media in the Making and Unmaking of the New Left* (Berkeley: University of California Press, 1980), 1. For a good critical account of the nature and role of the contemporary mass media, see Robert W. McChesney, *Rich Media, Poor Democracy: Communication Politics in Dubious Times* (Urbana and Chicago: University of Illinois Press, 1999).
4. On this, see Noam Chomsky, *Necessary Illusions: Thought Control in Democratic Societies* (Toronto: CBC Enterprises, 1989).
5. Ibid.
6. Thom Workman, *Banking on Deception: The Discourse of Fiscal Crisis* (Halifax: Fernwood Publishing, 1996), 32. This book provides an excellent treatment of how in the 1990s a powerful discourse on the 'evils' of government deficits and debt came to resonate with everyday conceptions of value people hold in a democratic capitalist culture such as Canada. See also Workman, "Hegemonic Modulation and the Discourse of Fiscal Crisis", *Studies in Political Economy* 59 (Summer 1999), 61–89.
7. Workman, "Hegemonic Modulation and the Discourse of Fiscal Crisis," 79ff.

8. Polling data compiled by Environics Research Group indicates that while in 1994, just before a federal budget that featured dramatic spending cuts in the interests of deficit reduction, 74 percent of those polled thought deficit reduction was very important, 30 percent defended maintaining existing program spending (versus 38 percent who argued that the deficit should be kept from increasing and 30 percent who argued against increasing taxes to support deficit reduction). I am grateful to Donna Dasko of Environics Research Group for providing me with this data, as well as the data cited in endnote 19, pg. 64.
9. To be sure, as suggested above such ideas do not emerge from nowhere. Groups and organizations with vested interests are often in the forefront in promoting them. This has been especially true with regard to the spread of neo-liberal ideas. For an account of how one policy think-tank participated in, and reflected, this process, see Alan Ernst, "From Liberal Continentalism to Neoconservatism: North American Free Trade and the Politics of the C.D. Howe Institute," *Studies in Political Economy* 39 (Autumn 1992), 109–40. Nonetheless, the ideas that emerge from such organizations assume an academic form and are intended to persuade through their rational content.
10. Those who have studied political theory or philosophy will recognize this as central to the debate about justice between Socrates and Thrasymachus in Plato's *Republic*. Socrates sought to *define* justice, to determine its meaning. For him, "justice" meant: that which was appropriate or suitable for each person. By contrast, Thrasymachus attempted to show how the term "justice" was *used*. He called "justice" the advantage of the stronger, i.e., those who ruled or held power. In effect, justice provided a cover, a way of rationalizing the ability of the stronger to do down the weaker.
What was at issue for Socrates and Thrasymachus was the question of whether ideas had meaning and truth in and of themselves, or whether they were labels for something else, and their truth lay in how, why and by whom they were used. This issue shaped the entire argument in the *Republic* and has had enormous consequences for Western political thought and Western culture as a whole. For an excellent discussion of the issues in the debate, see Pitkin, *Wittegenstein and Justice*, ch.VIII.
11. Standing behind this claim is that idea that society cannot be understood simply from the point of view of specific individuals alone. It has an objective character not explained solely by reference to our conscious, individual thoughts and actions or by our everyday subjective conceptions of what society as a whole might be. The question of exactly what society "is" involves important conceptual and philosophical issues beyond the scope of this study. For a good, brief summary of these issues, see David Frisby and Derek Sayer, *Society* (London and New York: Tavistock Publications, 1986).
12. C.B. Macpherson, "Problems of a Non-Market Theory of Democracy," in his *Democratic Theory: Essays in Retrieval* (Oxford: Clarendon Press, 1973), 51.
13. Canada is not alone in experiencing what might be called a "malaise" of democracy. For a thoughtful and suggestive treatment of this issue in the context of forces at work globally, see John Keane, "Whatever Happened to Democracy" (A public lecture delivered for the Institute for Public Policy Research, London, 27 March, 2002), available at www.wmin.ac.uk/esd/JKWhateverHappenedtoDemocracy.htm. See also the recently published Discussion Paper, *Renewing Democracy: Debating Electoral Reform in Canada*

22 / Taxing Illusions

   (Canada: Law Commission of Canada, 2002). Proponents of reforms such as proportional representation to elect members of legislative bodies usually formulate their proposals in light of a commitment to an expanded democratic political system.
14. Macpherson, "Problems..." 51. A more contemporary restatement of Macpherson's position here would have to take into account a range of issues he did not address, from the question of civil society to the nature of individual identities as these have been shaped by forces of gender, race and class. On such questions, see for example Chantel Mouffe, ed., *Dimensions of Radical Democracy: Pluralism, Citizenship, Community* (London: Verso, 1992); and Seyla Benhabib, ed., *Democracy and Difference: Contesting the Boundaries of the Political* (Princeton, NJ: Princeton University Press, 1996). But for my purposes here, it is the distinction Macpherson draws between these two understandings of democracy that is important because it illuminates the question of taxation. I would note, in addition, that, as will be seen later, Macpherson has an account of the relation of democracy to capitalism that is still valuable, not least because much contemporary democratic theory seems indifferent to it.
15. Frank Cunningham, a Canadian political philosopher influenced by Macpherson, has recently pursued the question of the meaning of democracy by developing an analysis of the different "degrees" of democracy in different social settings. Cunningham draws upon the ideas of the twentieth-century American philosopher, John Dewey, who viewed democracy not only as a narrowly political but also as a social idea, in terms of which people possessed the capacity to regulate the activities of the overlapping social groups to which they belonged. Democracy was about shaping the affairs of multiple "publics," and each "public," or site of collective activity, posed its own challenges and prospects for participatory engagement. Thus, "rather than regarding democracy as a quality that a social site either has or lacks, one should focus on 'publics' to ask how democratic (or undemocratic) they are, how democratic they might (or ought to) be, and how democracy within them can be enhanced." Clearly, Cunningham includes within the scope of his argument not only representative bodies but also other social and economic institutions, as well as the issues of identity raised in footnote 14. In this light, he professes sympathy with what he takes to be Dewey's, and Macpherson's, position "that a democratically functioning group is to be valued especially for liberating development of the potentialities of all the individuals in it." He also sympathizes with "the view of each theorist that egalitarian, and in Macpherson's case socialistic, policies are required for approximating this goal." Frank Cunningham, *Democratic Theory: A Critical Introduction* (London and New York: Routledge, 2002), 144, 143. It should be noted that Macpherson, himself, was critical of Dewey's theory of democracy. See Macpherson, *The Life and Times of Liberal Democracy* (Oxford: Oxford University Press, 1977), 73–5. I treat questions of democratic theory more extensively in Chapter Four.
16. John S. Dryzek, *Democracy in Capitalist Times: Ideals, Limits, and Struggles* (Oxford: Oxford University Press, 1996), 5.
17. For a brief review of recent provincial tax reform initiatives, see Geoffrey Hale, *The Politics of Taxation in Canada* (Peterborough: Broadview Press, 2002), 330ff.
18. The NDP government in power in Ontario from 1990 until 1995 did conduct a

comprehensive tax review through the Ontario Fair Tax Commission, which reported in 1993. However, when dramatic changes occurred in the provincial tax system, they came about after the election of a Progressive Conservative government in 1995 and represented a very different set of values and purposes from those which informed the report of the Fair Tax Commission.

For a brief review of the tax cutting ways of governments from across Canada in recent years and the extent of the cuts proposed and implemented, see Murray Campbell, "Have compassionate Canadians gone greedy?" *The Globe and Mail* (Toronto), May 6, 2000, A9.

19. Neo-liberal ideas are obviously central to the dominant ideological outlook of a capitalist society and so tend to be "in the air" without being specifically codified and stated. However, certain authors have gained fame and attention for specifically arguing and promoting them, notably Friedrich Hayek and Milton Friedman. In Canada, neo-liberal ideas were at the heart of the 1985 *Report of the Royal Commission on the Economic Union and Development Prospects for Canada* 3 vol. (Ottawa: Minister of Supply and Services, 1985) (the Macdonald Commission) which recommended continental free trade and provided the rationale for the Canada-U.S. Free Trade Agreement and, its successor, the North American Free Trade Agreement. (Steps are currently being taken to extend the latter in the form of a free trade agreement for the Americas, North and South.) According to Geoffrey Hale, neo-liberalism emerged in Canada because, from the nineteen seventies onward, "Canada's growing dependence on international markets, the growing awareness of the costs of economic inefficiencies created by fiscal and regulatory restrictions, and the effects of rapid technological change have led to new coalitions of producer and consumer groups pursuing a neo-liberal economic agenda. These have successfully pressured governments for economic deregulation, a retreat from interventionist nationalism, government initiatives to promote more rather than less competition, and a trend away from preferential tax treatment for particular industries." Hale, *The Politics of Taxation in Canada*, 74.

For a critical account of neo-liberalism and its policy consequences, particularly with regard to its impact on developing or underdeveloped countries, see Arthur MacEwan, *Neo-Liberalism or Democracy? Economic Strategy, Markets, and Alternatives for the 21st Century* (Halifax: Fernwood Publishing, 1999).

20. For analyses of this period, see Neil Bradford, "The Policy Influence of Economic Ideas: Interests, Institutions and Innovations in Canada," *Studies in Political Economy* 59 (Summer 1999), 17–60; and Robert M. Campbell, "The Fourth Fiscal Era: Can There Be a 'Post Neo-conservative' Fiscal Policy," in Leslie A. Pal, ed., *How Ottawa Spends 1999–2000: Shape Shifting Canadian Governance Toward the 21st Century* (Toronto: Oxford University Press, 1999), 113–49.

21. Canada, *Report of The Royal Commission on Taxation* (Ottawa: Queen's Printer, 1967).

22. This was certainly true of the Carter Commission. See my discussion of this in Chapter Two. For a more extensive treatment of the reception to the Commission's findings and recommendations, see Linda McQuaig, *Behind Closed Doors: How the Rich Won Control of Canada's Tax System and Ended Up Richer* (Toronto: Viking/Penguin, 1987).

Chapter Two

Taxation as an Expression of Community:
Report of the Saskatchewan Royal Commission on Taxation (1965)

The Saskatchewan Royal Commission on Taxation was established in 1963 in response to the Canadian federal government's own royal commission created the previous year.[1] It was headed by Thomas H. McLeod, who at that time was Dean of the College of Commerce at the University of Saskatchewan but who also enjoyed a lengthy and distinguished career as an important official in Cooperative Commonwealth Federation and, later, New Democratic Party governments. It issued its final report in May 1965. The Royal Commission study was comprehensive in scope. The Commission was mandated to consider and report upon "the systems of taxation which comprise the total tax structure in effect in the Province of Saskatchewan"[2] as well as the legal and administrative aspects of these systems. The Commission interpreted its terms broadly: it believed itself empowered "to inquire into any or all aspects of public policy which affect the flow of revenues into the general treasury of the province or into the coffers of its constituent local governing bodies."[3] It also attempted to range widely in the conduct of its inquiry. It conducted public hearings in Regina, and an extensive range of public and private sector organizations appeared before it. It mailed questionnaires to people throughout the province and received a significant number of responses. It commissioned research studies, with its research staff drawn from the University of Saskatchewan in Saskatoon, the only university then in existence in the province, as well as from other organizations with an interest in fiscal policy.[4]

The origin and focus of the Royal Commission reflected the era in which it was created and the then dominant approach to taxation and issues of public policy in general. The Great Depression of the 1930s, the demands of the Second World War, the pressures of post-war reconstruction and the consequent quest for both stable economic growth and social and economic equality had fostered the emergence of what has been called the Keynesian welfare state.[5] The ideas of Keynes supported a positive and interventionist role for governments in the economy. Through the use of both fiscal policy (taxing and spending) and monetary policy (interest rates, the money supply and exchange rates), governments could ensure continuing high levels of demand for goods and services and thus high levels of output and employment. These ideas first came to prominence during the worldwide Great Depression of the 1930s, when the capitalist system everywhere virtually collapsed as production fell drastically and unemployment rose to calamitous heights. Deep social misery and, in many countries, political unrest were the consequences of this crisis of capitalism. Keynes and those who followed in his wake believed the Great Depression demonstrated that by itself private enterprise could not successfully utilize all a community's resources and thus maintain economic wellbeing. They felt that by increasing the supply of money and, if necessary by borrowing, and when the economy was healthy, through taxation, governments could, and should, pick up the slack and employ resources the private sector could not. In other words, by purchasing goods and services and creating jobs in the public sector, that is, by fostering demand for products, labour and capital, governments could effectively ward off a depression. The economic successes of the wartime and post-war eras appeared to vindicate this position.

Pressures for equality, the other element in the rise of the Keynesian welfare state, were met with measures for income redistribution and the provision of certain services through social programs. In Canada, these included unemployment insurance, increasing public support for schools and post-secondary education, universal old age security and contributory public pensions, social assistance, and medical and hospital insurance. The tax system addressed the pursuit of both stable economic development and equality by facilitating macroeconomic regulation and, through its progressive rate structure, by raising the revenues to support social spending and income redistribution.[6]

By the early 1960s, two factors linked closely to the emergence of the Keynesian welfare state in Canada led to pressures for tax reform. One was the continued popular support for equality, which translated into a preference for greater tax fairness. The other was increasing competition between federal and provincial governments for resources as provincial budgets and program responsibilities grew. Although the federal government had led the way in building the welfare state and the post-war tax system that was an essential element of it, Canada's constitution places social policy primarily under provincial jurisdiction. The very development of the welfare state fostered the growth of stronger provincial governments and hence increasingly vigorous debate over access to tax revenues.[7]

In response to these pressures, in 1962, the Progressive Conservative federal government of John Diefenbaker established the Royal Commission on Taxation, with Toronto accountant, Kenneth Carter, as chair. Following extensive consultations and significant research contributions, the Commission, which reported in 1967, recommended a substantial overhaul of the federal tax system in the interests of greater equity. The Commission assumed that a tax system should address what it called "gains in discretionary economic power,"[8] by which it meant increases in individual net wealth over the course of a taxable period. It therefore recommended a substantially broadened income tax base that would include not only income from employment but also increases in the value of assets. In effect, it argued that all income was alike and should be treated alike; hence the slogan "a buck is a buck," with which the Royal Commission came to be identified. Out of its commitment to equity, the Carter Commission therefore recommended the taxation of capital gains, that is, increases in the value of assets, which had not before then been subject to taxation.

Supporters and critics viewed the changes proposed by the Carter Commission as momentous. According to Geoffrey Hale, the recommendations would have exposed "for the first time virtually all areas of economic activity and private property to direct taxation by the federal government." In particular, "Carter's proposals to tax investment income on an accrual basis [i.e., on the basis of increases in the value of assets] would have prevented the growth of large concentrations of wealth and economic power in private hands and facilitated its redistribution by governments to less fortunate Canadians or, alternatively, its transfer to government control."[9]

Although the Carter Commission report exhibited a significant egalitarian thrust, it was unlikely even at the time, that implementing it would produce sweeping or radical consequences. Carter, himself, accepted the private accumulation of unequal holdings of wealth.[10] Nonetheless, that it could be viewed this way *and that the supposedly radical claims with which it was identified were considered at least relevant to serious public debate* tells us something about how equality held a significant place in the political discourse of the era.

In the event, vocal and sustained opposition to the Royal Commission by business and financial interests resulted in a substantial watering down of the Commission's recommendations (although commitment to greater equity nominally remained central to the rationale for tax reform).[11] A subsequent government white paper on tax reform in 1969 and federal tax legislation enacted in 1971 were shadows of the Carter Report. In the end, a limited capital gains tax imposed upon the sale of an asset was introduced, although this was later to some extent offset by the gradual elimination, federally and provincially, of estate taxes and succession duties (i.e., inheritance taxes). Modified over time, the tax system set in place by the 1971 legislation remains to this day.

The McLeod Commission in Saskatchewan was rather more modest in its scope. Unlike the Carter Commission, it did not propose a substantially reconstructed tax system, although it did recommend changes to certain specific taxes (most controversially, the replacement of local property taxes by provincial revenues to fund education and social service programs). At the same time, however, it held and articulated many of the same assumptions and political values about the nature and place of taxation. In this respect, it provides a clear perspective on the role of the state in the economy and society and so offers a picture of the political culture of the Keynesian era.

The Saskatchewan in which the McLeod Commission was created had, under the populist and social democratic CCF government in power since 1944, become in many respects the model of the Canadian version of the Keynesian welfare state. It featured an activist government staffed by a capable, indeed nationally and internationally renowned, body of public servants, which generated innovative public policies. This was particularly true in the area of social policy, most notably Saskatchewan's hospital and medical insurance programs, which provided the standard for the national programs that were subsequently established. On the economic policy front, the government engaged in economic planning and used public investment through Crown corporations in a number of areas (although over the course of its stay in office, it tended to shy away from this alternative, in part because of high profile failures with public investment in manufacturing enterprises during its early years in office). To be sure, the cooperative and private sectors played central roles in promoting economic development; although labelled "socialist" by its political foes, the CCF government did not seek to supplant private capital. Nonetheless, its economic role was significant, especially by contemporary standards.

Politically, the CCF was, in Canadian terms, a mass party with a large and active membership. The party saw itself, and presented itself, as the democratic voice of its supporters—small farmers and urban workers—and the vehicle for achieving their aspirations. This required a central role for the state, as the body in society most capable of carrying out the popular will. To a considerable degree, CCF governments at least shared in this view. Woodrow S. Lloyd, the Premier of Saskatchewan when the McLeod Commission was established, clearly expressed it:

> I believe in government.... It is a belief based on the fact that democratic government operating through parliamentary procedures is the most effective method of implementing the conscious will of the people.... Properly used it results in a part for the individual which is not diminished but enhanced.[12]

Because Saskatchewan was a small jurisdiction occupying a subordinate position in a capitalist political economy, the province typically supported a strong role for the federal government. The provincial government needed an active federal administration capable both of redistributing income between groups and regions and of managing the national economy in the interests of continuing high levels of growth.[13]

These factors found their place in the logic and arguments of the McLeod Commission. In part this came through in what the Commission took for granted. Much of this is striking because it stands in contrast to views widely proclaimed today, especially by governments and business. For example, the Commission did not engage in either substantive policy evaluation or assessment of administrative efficiency. For it, the revenue generating responsibilities of the state merited autonomous consideration precisely because sound public policy and effective administration were taken as given, as expressions for the necessary role of the state in society. (This is in contrast to the current view that government is inherently inefficient and must be "reinvented" using private sector-style strategies associated with what has been called "The New Public Management"[14]). Indeed, the Commission assumed that the then current pattern of public policies and financial demands needed to maintain it would continue. Such policies were thought to reflect the public will and therefore so did tax policies: "Tax programs of governments must be consonant with, or at least not in opposition to the social philosophy of the community as it is reflected in the policies of its governments."[15]

The Commission viewed this matter as especially critical because while

> revenue policies of governments should produce the necessary funds to meet their regular commitments, that is by no means the end of the matter.... Tax laws are not designed simply as vehicles for raising money ... [since] ... considerations other than the raising of money do enter in: redistribution of the community's income; the securing of "adequate" contributions from users of particular facilities or services; control of the level, if not the direction, of consumer spending; encouragement, discouragement or direction of investment; these and many other considerations must be weighed.[16]

The Commission assumed both a strong public desire for public services and, just as importantly, *a general willingness to pay for such services through taxation.* Of course to varying degrees taxes are always "unpopular" and viewed as "burdensome." But this is "conventional wisdom" the Commission felt compelled and able to challenge. It assumed that, in doing so, it would make sense to its audience, that its criticism of conventional wisdom would seem plausible. The Commission addressed this issue in two ways: through a general claim about the overall commitment of resources in a community and through suggestions about the appropriate mix of specific taxes.

Interestingly, the Commission viewed the place of taxation and the question of "tax burden" in relation to the wants and needs of the provincial community and not within the framework of individual incentives and choices alone. To be sure, the Commission did not completely slight "individualist" claims, while it did state that, in the course of its inquiry, it found no evidence of a general sense that existing taxes were burdensome.

The Commission suggested that this "indicates, rather a judgment that existing relationships between aggregate tax costs and aggregate social benefits is, on the whole, a satisfactory one."[17]

More significantly, the Commission claimed that the very idea of a tax burden is misleading if it is meant simply or solely to describe increases in tax effort and revenue or increases in taxation as a proportion of disposable income. In its view, "what these movements mean in terms of 'tax burden' is much more difficult to say, for accompanying these increases have been similar increases in the benefits provided through social expenditures to the community." Nor are matters substantially different if the tax burden question is treated comparatively. According to the Commission, "it is a fallacious proposition that differentials in rates between jurisdictions may be taken in themselves as measures of differential tax burdens.... Comparative tax costs, like other costs, can be determined only when a clear relationship is established with benefits derived."[18]

Here, the Commission outlined what is perhaps its key argument about tax policy, and fiscal policy generally. It asserted that the idea that taxes were burdensome *per se* "is derived from the notion that money accumulated by governments through its various taxing devices represents a net withdrawal of economic satisfactions from the community." This notion "is palpably nonsensical." There was no "rational basis" for the view that "government expenditures must enter the income stream in a different fashion from private expenditure or in some fashion have a different and less salutary effect on the economy."[19]

This is a significant and powerful claim, all the more so because it stands at odds with much current ideology about the role of the state and the nature of economic life. The Commission here was defending the view that governments were not just parasites draining resources from the private sector, supposedly the only source of "real" value and wealth. Rather, the government, the public sector, contributed to economic, and not just social, wellbeing in its own right. It performed a positive function. This was not restricted to aiding private sector activity. Nor was it to be understood in terms of a currently widespread tendency to contrast "equity" with "efficiency." Because of the place this contrast now occupies in contemporary political discourse, it is worth exploring here a bit further.

Equity is typically understood as state "interference" with private sector, market driven activities, whereby governments use social spending, taxation and regulation of business and industry to achieve a more equal distribution of both individual life chances and material resources. Applied specifically to taxation, this is often seen as involving two dimensions: horizontal equity (as between different kinds of income, such as wages and capital gains) and vertical equity (as between different and unequal income groups). By contrast, efficiency refers to the use of society's resources in a way that avoids waste; typically this involves the notion that resources are being efficiently used where no one can be made better off without making someone else worse off. More specifically, it involves the idea that the decisions governing the use of resources should reflect people's individual choices, and only where it does so can we be certain that what is produced is what is really wanted and therefore needed. Since, it is claimed, only the market can successfully reveal people's true preferences, only the wealth producing activities of the private sector can be fully efficient.

It has become almost a given in contemporary political and policy circles that, not only are considerations of efficiency more fundamental, but equity measures inherently diminish efficiency, so that there is always a trade off between them.[20] The implication is that strong arguments have to be made on behalf of equity because of the potential threat to efficiency this poses. "Free" market critics of the welfare state assume this position, but so do most contemporary defenders of redistributive social policies. It reflects the current dominance of neo-liberal ideas about the inherent superiority of markets. But as I hope to show, it also suggests something more: a certain conception of the nature of the individual and what individual wellbeing consists of. The free market assumption is that our wellbeing revolves around preferences for certain things that can only or primarily emerge in the marketplace and which are expressed through buying and selling.[21]

Given the nature of a modern capitalist society organized around states and markets, the issue of equity versus efficiency is always at least implicitly present. But it becomes particularly explicit, and even a matter of political debate, when state and market are viewed as inherently and necessarily separate and when it is believed that the market needs protection from the state. This, essentially, is the case today.

But it wasn't the case in the Keynesian era, when the McLeod Commission prepared its study. The Commission could thus assume that its claim about the positive role of government could be readily defended in the prevailing context of widely held social and political values. In other words, it appeared to believe that the production of wealth was a complex social process in which both states and markets were indispensable. Governments did not just correct market outcomes, for good or ill. This assumed that only the private sector engaged in productive economic activity, which governments could either facilitate or block, but not generate. The Commission seemed to think otherwise.

It did not explicitly lay this out. But its analysis resonated with the argument made by the American political scientist, Charles Lindblom, in his now classic study, *Politics and Markets*.

> One of the great misconceptions of conventional economic theory is that businessmen are induced to perform their functions by purchases of their goods and services, as though the vast productive tasks performed in market-oriented systems could be motivated

solely by exchange relations between buyers and sellers. On so slender a foundation no great productive system could be established. What is required in addition is a set of governmentally provided inducements in the form of market and political benefits. And because market demands themselves do not spontaneously spring up, they too have to be nurtured by government. Governments in market-oriented societies systems have always been busy with these necessary activities.[22]

Reinforcing this point in a slightly different way, Lindblom also noted that "in any private enterprise system, a large category of major decisions is turned over to businessmen [sic], both small and larger. They are taken off the agenda of government. Businessmen thus become a kind of public official and exercise what, on a broad view of their role, are public functions."[23] The boundary separating public from private sectors was not so sharp as is commonly claimed today.

It was perhaps because this connection between governments and markets was widely accepted that the Commission found little evidence of major dissatisfaction with existing overall levels of taxation. In fact, it foresaw a necessary growth in tax revenues to fund more adequately existing programs and services. This would involve both increases in the size of government budgets and increases in the proportion of the income of the community devoted to public purposes. The Commission found "no reason to assume, in light of the projected economic circumstances, that the community will not be able to bear this increase with the same relative lack of difficulty that it has borne past increases. *There is even less reason to assume it will be unwilling to do so.*"[24] There seemed, in other words, to be significant acceptance of an extensive state presence in the society.

And the Commission envisaged the prospect of an even greater role for the state in the years to come, particularly in a province that had been devastated by the Great Depression and had undergone rebuilding during the post-war economic boom. It wrote: "In purely economic terms it could even be argued that in a community which is still a developing one, a yet greater proportion of the community's income might with good effect be devoted to the creation of basic infrastructure." In light of this, the Commission concluded—again, note the differences from today—that "the existing tax system is far from being confiscatory in its impact."[25]

The Commission did argue that the tax structure of the province might at some point have to be altered in response to the needs and demands of the community:

> it will be necessary for the governments of the province to consider tax-rate *increases* as well as tax-rate decreases.... Our expenditure projections would indicate that apart from major reductions in the

level of services provided or the appearance of new major revenue sources which are not at present apparent, there is little that can be offered, permanently to the community in the way of a major reduction in the level of its tax bill. It must also be added that further expressions of preference for communal expenditure in new or extended social programs will serve to add to it.[26]

Given its perspective on the question of tax burden, it is reasonable to assume the Commission viewed the prospect of maintaining or even enhancing existing tax revenue with equanimity. But—and this relates to the second dimension of its response—it made clear that any shifts in the tax mix would have to be considered carefully. To be sure, it is not uncommon for current proponents of tax "reform" to suggest tax increases along with tax decreases. However, proposed increases are almost invariably tied to consumption taxes, based on what people spend, as opposed to income or capital levies, based upon what they earn or own.

For its part, the Commission did not necessarily disagree with the idea of changes to certain taxes, although it cautioned against "tinkering" with particular taxes as opposed to considering the revenue-generating system as a whole.[27] But it made clear that such changes were never merely technical or neutral. Nor were they to be viewed, as is common nowadays, from the sole perspective of the allegedly unchallengeable requirements of the market and its allocation of resources. It was "exceptionally difficult to arrive at any definitive conclusions as to the adequacy or equity of any particular type of tax levied." Perspective or context was vital for evaluating different taxes. For instance, a *per capita* tax could be viewed either as a regressive poll tax or an essential user's fee. Much depended on the answer to the question, "how much of a social service may appropriately be charged to a user without affronting broadly accepted principles of community responsibility for certain easily accessible services for all?"[28] The issue involved more than the requirements of efficiency. It was also a matter of equity, even equality, and hence community: how should the community, with its evident commitment to public provisioning, ensure accessibility to services which all ought to receive as a matter of right?

What linked together the Commission's position on overall resource use in the community to specific tax choices and hence its challenge to conventional wisdom about tax burdens was its explicit support of "the principle that taxation is most equitable, and therefore most defensible, when it is based upon ... ability to pay."[29] For the Commission, ability to pay entailed "the principle of progression within the tax structure." This required "that as individual means increase beyond the point at which they are sufficient to provide for basic human needs, however defined, they may be taxed with *increasing stringency without loss of equity*."[30] There is strongly implied here an argument for steeply graduated marginal rates of taxation at higher levels of income, an idea rarely entertained these days, even by defenders of progressive taxation. More significantly, the Commission echoed the arguments of the Carter Commission in claiming that by itself, income was not the sole, nor for the purpose of determining means, always the most adequate way to measure ability to pay. Gifts or capital gains also contributed to the growth of personal wealth and had to be taken into account in establishing an equitable tax regime.[31]

So for the Commission, the matter of tax burdens was complex. It could not be explored independently of questions of community and the just and equitable allocation of resources within it. To be sure, the Commission did not challenge the central role or value of individual freedom to choose. It did, however, take issue with the view that such choices are made only privately through individual purchases in the marketplace. Choices were also public, exercised collectively through the state. As we have seen, the Commission argued that public spending decisions and the means to finance them reflected community preferences. Indeed, it is only if they did not do so or if the community did not receive full value for the money spent that one might speak of an undue tax burden. But even here, "No assessment of either possibility can be made on any *a priori* basis, nor is there anything in brute statistics which will reveal a ready answer."[32]

In any event, the Commission was inclined to view existing programs and services and the taxation needed to pay for them as broadly reflecting community preferences. Hence any burdens were self-imposed. The Commissioners claimed they were "satisfied that at least rough justice is done if individual tax payments bear some equitable relationship to total available individual means for their payment."[33]

To be sure, as is common today, the Commission was apt to label individuals exercising choices as "consumers," whether these choices were private or public. Yet it may not have been totally comfortable with its own choice of terms here. The Report put "consumer" in quotation marks and distinguished "communal" from "private" forms of expenditure.[34] Given the language used, it at least implied that the two were not identical and could not be assimilated one to the other.

This is not just a technical issue, but points to a critical question: what is the nature of the citizen/taxpayer? The Commission made what might seem a minor point but in fact is substantial: "taxes are levied, ultimately if not in the first instance, against people and not against things."[35] While it noted the importance of recognizing this in the context of property and sales taxes, where it might appear that things were being taxed, the Commission was on to something more significant. It stressed this point because it wanted to make as clear as possible exactly who paid a specific tax. In part this permitted "consumers" to know what their tax bills would be, so that they could make rational choices about communal expenditures. But the Commission also noted that modes of taxation that obscured rather than revealed who paid taxes made it difficult to determine for such "unknown" taxpayers whether or not it was fairly within their capacity to pay the tax demanded of them.[36]

The critical point here is that while we normally speak of "individual tax payers," and tax studies typically assume that individuals exercise choice, even if for different things based upon differences in resources and preferences, in reality there is no single rationally choosing individual who can be considered apart from social ties. Individuals are socially located. They have concrete identities shaped in significant ways by class, ethnicity, race and gender. They possess distinctive life histories—think of the situation of a typical working person as opposed to that of a wealthy businessperson or powerful political figure—and encounter different circumstances during the course of their everyday lives. This is likely to affect how they experience and view the world and its possibilities. Especially important for our purposes here, they bear significantly different relations to an unequal economic order that distributes resources, opportunities and outcomes in a highly differentiated, patterned and ongoing way. In a society that puts a premium on "making it," not everyone can or will, and this is not merely, or in most cases even primarily, because of individual failings. Whether one wishes to justify or criticize it, material inequality is a fundamental feature of a capitalist market society. It relates to how society is organized and not just to individual choices and decisions. This must inform any account of taxation policy.

In this light, the concept of "income" itself must be understood as more than cash income:

> Personal real incomes in a community with well developed services are obviously greater than those of a community where such services do not exist, even though cash incomes (and the pattern of their distribution) are identical. To the extent that personal benefits are derived from public expenditures, and it is obvious that they are, incomes and total means are altered.[37]

In line with the implication that the nature of the individual citizen/consumer is by no means a simple matter, the Commission here in effect argued that personal wellbeing had a collective, material dimension that cannot be defined by cash holdings alone. In other words, wellbeing included more that the goods and services, or the ability to acquire these, that one might individually obtain through buying and selling, that is, through engagement in market relations. Taxation policy must take this into account, too.

At the end of the day, questions of taxation and its "burdens" must ultimately be addressed "in the area of practical politics and day-to-day public administration."[38] Decisions about what proportion of its income a community commits to collective provisioning are appropriately made through the political process. It would make little sense, for example, to speak in the abstract of existing taxes being too high. "There is no 'magic number' that can be prescribed as the theoretical limit to the level of taxation." To be sure, there may at any point in time be a limit to communal versus private spending. "But the proportionate relationship of these choices changes over time. We have all seen them change drastically with changes in the ideas of the community as to how its money may best be spent. As a result, new limits are set."[39]

It is also worth noting there was no claim here that the issue fundamentally involved a question that looms large these days with respect to tax policies: how to provide individuals with incentives. Central to this idea is that individuals are essentially self-interested and self-regarding and that they must be induced or persuaded to engage in economic activity by the prospect of personal gain, understood as the ability to acquire command over goods and services.

There seem to be two senses in which the idea of incentives is used. In general terms, taxes are held to be disincentives because work is burdensome—to use the language of economists, it has disutility—and people will only do it if they are amply rewarded for their efforts. Taxes cut into these rewards. More specifically, the issue of incentives is typically linked to the idea that those who own capital, that is, possess funds for investment, will not invest unless encouraged by a market-friendly tax system.

The notion that there is a problem of incentives has become especially fashionable in recent years as part of the emergence of neo-liberalism and its emphasis on the primary place of the market in economic life. The market aggregates individual choices, with choice, itself, conceived as the expression of self-interest. Given the assumption that self-interest alone drives economic activity, only the private, market-based sector of the economy can foster growth. If the operation of market forces is discouraged, economic decline ensues. As will be discussed in the next chapter, the period after 1975 in particular has been one of less secure and less stable economic growth; this is the period in which there has been the turn to neo-liberalism.

In the Keynesian era, when the Commission did its work, the issue of incentives did not figure. In its analysis, the Commission gave no indication that, in its view, there was an obvious or transparent connection between taxation and individual productive effort. As has already been indicated, the Commission denied that existing taxes were confiscatory; it also defended a complex conception of wellbeing.

Now, the members of the Commission were not political theorists. They did not provide, nor intend to offer, a critical treatment of abstract, individual "choosers." Nor did they give an account of socially "located" individuals—or embedded agents, to use a current term. Nonetheless, their approach to taxation stands out because of what it assumed about collective life in a capitalist market society. In the eyes of the Commission, state expenditures, indeed a significant role for the state in the economy and society generally, had legitimacy. In this light, the Commission brought forth a reasonably sophisticated, if abbreviated, account of the changing role of the state over time. In the process, it also referred to the issue of individualism:

> The degree to which the government enters the arena of economic decisionmaking is not likely to decline. The breadth of government activity in economic life is a function not only of political philosophy but also—and in large measure—of the changing needs of an industrializing society. Historical evidence supports the conclusion that greater *inter*dependence, rather than greater *in*dependence, among the citizenry is the consequence of economic development.[40]

I have already noted the Commission's view that state expenditures would likely have to increase to fund existing and projected demands for public services. In fact, its conception of the role of the state was set out against the backdrop of revenue forecasts for the period to 1972. However, just as taxation was about more than raising revenue, so the changing role of the state, which undergirded changing taxation regimes, had implications for more than the size of government budgets. The Commission also related the expanded and expanding place of the state to two fundamental issues: the nature of and prospects for economic development and the appropriate place of overall fiscal policy in the response of governments to the demands of economic growth. In both respects, what the Commission had to say stands out against current contemporary views on these questions.

Just as the Commissioners were not political theorists, telling us explicitly about the nature of the individual, the state and the community, so they were not political economists either. They did not elaborate a detailed account of the institutions of organized economic activity and the relation of these to political forces and bodies. At the same time, however, they hinted at such an account in that their discussion of economic growth was informed by a sense of context and history, both indispensable for a dynamic treatment of economic institutions and political processes.

It is interesting that the Report specifically took issue with the current dominant assumption that tax rates, and in particular income tax rates, constitute a primary, if not the most important, factor determining the location of private investment capital. To be sure, the Commission noted that, during the course of its deliberations,

> it was contended on more than one occasion that within the existing tax system, the income taxes above all others are those which most

affect investment decisions. *Even after having given due weight to the possibility of special pleading in this matter*, we have concluded that if there is, because of comparative tax structures, a sensitive area in the making of marginal calculations related to investment, it lies in the area of income taxes.[41]

However, the cautious and tentative language suggests the Commission was reluctant to attribute to comparative differences in income tax rates the determining economic role claimed by much contemporary analysis. Here, the Commission's sense of context came into play. It understood it was examining the economy of Saskatchewan, a polity with a particular history and location within the national and international economy.

As a result, the Commission was careful and conservative in its predictions about future economic growth in the province. Growth there would be, and according to the Report, it would be carried by an expansion of resource-based and other activities, with the role of agriculture, in a traditionally agrarian province, declining in significance (this turned out to be prophetic). But Saskatchewan would continue to have *per capita* income at levels below the national average, unless the shift from lower productivity agriculture to higher productivity non-agricultural employment appreciably accelerated.[42]

In light of these projections, the Commission foresaw significant strains on public finance. It believed the cost of government would increase at a rate faster than would provincial income. As noted above, the Commission felt these strains could be managed in that the community had indicated a willingness to sustain current and even prospectively higher levels of public expenditure on programs and services. Given the situation, it cautioned that if there was a move to a general reduction in taxes, this could only come about either through "a reduction in the level of demand for public services [which the Commission had already largely ruled out], or alternatively, as the result of an increase greater than that which at the moment seems likely to take place in the income available to the community."[43]

Contemporary fiscal wisdom would dictate that tax cuts, coupled with expenditure reductions, would boost growth and cure the problem. Such ideas found little favour with the Commission. From its perspective, this approach would be ineffective because it failed to consider the characteristics of Saskatchewan as a political and economic unit. The words of the Report spell this out:

> To the extent that it is within the power of a provincial government to operate effectively in inducing economic activity, the most likely route to achievement of this objective is not to be found, in our opinion, in any program of unilateral tax adjustment. Policies to be followed by the province, in this respect, must be *of a more positive*

and substantial nature. We could find little empirical evidence ... that provincial taxation policies are more than marginal elements in the making of economic decisions that most affect our rate of growth and development.... Any disabilities which Saskatchewan may exhibit in the matter of economic development rest primarily upon its disadvantages in areas other than tax policies: markets, transportation costs, available industrial water, cheap energy supply, and similar considerations. Provincial tax policies are, at worst, a residual element in the picture, and the element least likely to affect business decisions.... [W]ithin the complexities of the Canadian economy and its appended tax structure, any provincial government acting alone and seeking through its tax structure to affect major economic purposes is likely to achieve its end only by accident.[44]

This is a striking passage. The claims of the Commission stand clearly at odds with currently dominant ideas about the economic role of government. As will be seen in the examination of the more recent tax review in Saskatchewan, the dominant theme now is that taxation policy is virtually the *only* means a provincial government has to foster economic growth. And as indicated above and pursued below, this view is based on certain assumptions about individual behaviour and the nature of society that fly in the face of the historical and institutional approach of the Commission. Its approach sustained the claim that economic development required policies "of a more positive and substantial nature" than those associated with tax reductions alone. Such positive and substantial policies evidently included public spending, investment and regulation of the sort not often considered these days.

It would of course be misleading to claim that the Commission proposed a fundamental modification of the role played by markets and the private sector in allocating resources, at least during the period when the Commission did its work. (By contemporary standards, what then seemed normal and appropriate now appears much more radical and heterodox.) But its analysis challenged any view which failed to appreciate that economic decisionmaking was the outcome of a complex array of factors, of which taxation was only one.

However, while it might have accepted the central role of markets in general, the Commission nonetheless defended the need for significant government intervention. This was not only a matter of supporting specific economic initiatives either through direct public investment or expenditures on behalf of the private and cooperative sectors. It also included a commitment to sound, general economic management. Such management was viewed as critical because of the vulnerability of a capitalist market economy to the business cycle, that is, boom and bust, or dramatic swings in output and employment. "*We assume that we need not argue the case for government responsibility in the matters of counter cyclical control and persistent economic growth.* Nor should it be necessary to argue about the need for the measures and the mechanisms which will make both short and longer-run economic controls effective."[45]

In part for this reason, the Report devoted considerable attention to federal-provincial fiscal arrangements, that is, those agreements negotiated by the federal and provincial governments to determine how the tax powers of each level of government are to be exercised and tax revenues shared. We have already seen that the impetus for the creation of the McLeod Commission was the federal government's own efforts at tax reform and that, historically, the people and government of Saskatchewan favoured a strong role for the federal government in managing the national economy. Both of these factors found a place in the Commission's deliberations. In the early 1960s, federal and provincial governments had negotiated significant changes to fiscal arrangements, which resulted in a more decentralized system.[46] The Commission believed this would complicate, and perhaps even compromise, the tasks of economic management, what the Commission called "national economic control."[47] It therefore recommended that the government pursue the creation of new inter-governmental machinery for the integration and coordination of fiscal policies nationwide. Such a move would clearly be necessary because, through the imposition of their own personal and corporate income taxes, the provinces would now play a much more significant role in shaping the national economy.

In light of its wide-ranging concerns for both the historical and future economic position of Saskatchewan and the management of the national economy, the Commission ultimately believed that economic policy could not, and should not, be reduced to tax policy, least of all a policy based on the assumption that taxes were inherently "bad" and should be cut as quickly as possible. The wellbeing of the community, to which both private and public expenditures contributed, was paramount. The Commissioners believed those who appeared before them, or responded to the circulated questionnaire, agreed with them. They stated: "we have no reason to assume that the people of the province are likely to settle for any level of services below that now being provided." While some administrative efficiencies in the delivery of programs might be realized, the "most important factor in the picture is likely to remain the rate at which aggregate output and income in the province rise in comparison both with similar increases in Canada and, more importantly, in comparison with the wishes of the community to maintain its level of social expenditures."[48]

This factor, and the tax "burden" associated with it, must be related to the stage and level of economic development in the society, the conditions facilitating this development, and the role of taxation and the public sector in securing it. As noted previously, the Commission argued that, "it must be emphasized that the expenditure of ... funds provides for the basic 'infrastructure,' which is the necessary basis of any major economic development."[49] The Commission does not define "infrastructure," but in principle there is no barrier to a broad construal of it.

In fact, the Commission's position suggests critical questions about state policy. Is this claim as true of Saskatchewan—or any other liberal democratic capitalist state—now as the Commission argued it was then? Does the meaning of "infrastructure" change historically with patterns of political, social and economic development? What notions of wellbeing are involved here? Ultimately, because of the increasingly powerful impact of economic activities and forces on social life and the need to address this, does a capitalist economy require more state intervention as it matures? Given that the Commission report encourages such questions, it bears attention now, especially in an era in which such questions are rarely, if ever, posed by policymakers.

What are we to make of the McLeod Commission? Clearly, this was not a radical body, nor was its report a radical document. The Commissioners, themselves, were members of the community who held positions that normally command respect: aside from the Chair, who was Dean of Commerce at the University of Saskatchewan, there were two other members, a chartered accountant and a lawyer. As noted above, a wide range of public and private sector organizations appeared at its public hearings. Its research studies sat squarely in the mainstream of fiscal policy analysis.

In a way, that is the point: the McLeod Commission reflected the then prevalent "conventional wisdom." The importance of this was less in the specifics of their account or in their recommendations, which were unexceptional both in terms of the historical period and the kind of treatment accorded the taxation issue that one normally expects to see in a report of this sort. It lay, rather, in the assumptions informing the study and the way in which the Commission raised issues and argued its case. It lay, in other words, in the language and texture of the Report, in what it seemed to defend and take for granted. Specifically, the Commission treated taxation from the perspective of the relation between public expenditures and public wants and needs. It did not restrict its focus to the supposed economic role of taxation, that is, its alleged burdens on individuals, but forged its analysis on the basis of an attempt to relate the necessary and active role of government to society. There was, speaking broadly, an emphasis on institutions and their historical development. There was also a conception of the community and its requirements and purposes clearly visible at the core of the analysis. Above all, taxation was treated not simply as a regrettable, if unavoidable, cost but as an essential contribution to the wellbeing of all, taxpayers included, *and could, at least in principle, be defended on that basis.* In both what was said, and in how it was said, the *Report of the Royal Commission on Taxation* illuminated key

Taxation as an Expression of Community / 41

assumptions and commitments associated with the era of the Keynesian welfare state.

When the Government of Saskatchewan next undertook an extensive public review of the tax system in the province, the result was something very different.

Notes

1. A primary purpose of the Commission was: "To consult and co-operate with the Royal Commission on Taxation appointed by the Government of Canada, and to consider and report upon matters arising out of such consultations." Province of Saskatchewan, *Report of the Royal Commission on Taxation* (Regina: Queen's Printer, 1965), vi. (Hereafter referred to as *Report…*)
2. Ibid., vi.
3. Ibid., 3.
4. This information is drawn from Ibid., 244–7.
5. For an excellent and comprehensive account of the post-war era in Canada, with a particular focus on the socio-economic and political forces at work in Canadian society, see Alvin Finkel, *Our Lives: Canada after 1945* (Toronto: James Lorimer & Company Ltd., 1997).
6. For a general treatment of the rise (and subsequent crisis) of the welfare state from an historical, theoretical and comparative perspective, see Christopher Pierson, *Beyond the Welfare State: The New Political Economy of Welfare* Second Edition (University Park, PA: The Pennsylvania State University Press, 1998). For accounts of the welfare state in Canada, see, e.g., Greg M. Olsen, *The Politics of the Welfare State: Canada, Sweden, and the United States* (Don Mills, ON: Oxford University Press, 2002); Stephen McBride and John Shields *Dismantling a Nation: The Transition to Corporate Rule in Canada* Second Edition (Halifax: Fernwood Publishing, 1997), esp. ch.2; and Dennis Guest, *The Emergence of Social Security in Canada* 3rd edition (Vancouver: University of British Columbia Press, 1997).
   It should be pointed out that, as with all important thinkers, Keynes' ideas have been subject to diverse interpretations. The interpretation noted here which essentially identifies Keynes with what is called macroeconomic stabilization, that is, the use of fiscal and monetary policy to ensure stable growth, became the dominant view of his work. But there is also a more radical interpretation of Keynes, which stresses more strongly the tendency of a capitalist economy to fall prey to stagnation, i.e., low or nonexistent growth and consequently high unemployment. The emphasis here was more explicitly on the inability of the private sector by itself, even with supportive government policies, to generate continuing growth. In the circumstances, there was the need for extensive public investment and in general state economic planning. The fact that this interpretation lost out to the narrower emphasis on fiscal policy and, especially during the years of dramatic growth during the nineteen fifties and sixties, the fine tuning of an otherwise healthy private economy, itself raises important historical and political questions.
7. W. Irwin Gillespie, *Tax, Borrow and Spend: Financing Federal Spending in Canada, 1867–1990* (Ottawa: Carleton University Press, 1990), 185–6. In *The Politics of Taxation in Canada*, Geoffrey Hale contends interestingly that the

42 / Taxing Illusions

pressures for tax reform in the 1960s came from "tax professionals" acting on behalf of upper-income Canadians who feared that in cases involving disputes over taxes owed, the courts of the time were moving toward a more and more sweeping definition of taxable income that would result in punitive retroactive liabilities for wealthy tax payers (149–50). Of course this is another way of identifying popular pressures for greater equality: allegedly, even a conservative institution like the court system was becoming a vehicle for carrying out egalitarian policies.

8. Canada, Report..., 45.
9. Hale, *The Politics of Taxation in Canada*, 43, 52.
10. Carter and the Commission were strongly influenced by the ideas of an American economist and tax theorist, Henry Simon, who supported a progressive tax structure based on taxable income that included both consumption and savings, but who also staunchly defended private enterprise and competitive markets. Indeed he developed many of his ideas during the Great Depression as an alternative to pressures for socialism, which he feared and resisted. For a statement of his key ideas, see his *Personal Taxation: The Definition of Income as a Problem of Fiscal Policy* (1938) (Chicago & London: The University of Chicago Press, 1965).
11. For an account of the opposition mounted by business and financial interests, see Robert Gardner, "Tax Reform and Class Interests: The Fate of Progressive Reform, 1967–72," *Canadian Taxation* Vol.3, No.4 (Winter 1981), 245–57. Interestingly, one of the most vocal critics of Carter-inspired tax reform was the current Canadian media magnate, Israel Asper, who in the 1960s was a prominent tax lawyer. See Israel H. Asper, *The Benson Iceberg: A Critical Analysis of the White Paper on Tax Reform in Canada* (Toronto: Clarke, Irwin and Co., 1970). The White Paper referred to in the title was the federal government's response to the Carter Report.
12. W.S. Lloyd, "The Positive Role of Government," *Canadian Public Administration* (December 1962), 404–5; cited in M. Brownstone, "The Douglas-Lloyd Governments: Innovation and Bureaucratic Adaptation," in Laurier LaPierre et.al., eds., *Essays on the Left: Essays in Honour of T.C. Douglas* (Toronto/Montreal: McClelland and Stewart Limited, 1971), 65.
13. For accounts of the CCF era in Saskatchewan politics see, for example, Brownstone, "The Douglas-Lloyd Governments...", Lorne A. Brown, Joseph K. Roberts and John W.Warnock, *Saskatchewan Politics from Left to Right '44–'99* (Regina: Hinterland Publications, 1999); Christopher Dunn and David Laycock, "Saskatchewan: Innovation and Competition in the Agricultural Heartland," in Keith Brownsey and Michael Howlett, eds., *The Provincial State: Politics in Canada's Provinces and Territories* (Mississauga, ON: Copp Clark Pitman, 1992), 207–42; Evelyn Eager, *Saskatchewan Government: Politics and Pragmatism* (Saskatoon: Western Producer Books, 1980); Ken Rasmussen, "Saskatchewan: From Entrepreneurial State to Embedded State," in Keith Brownsey and Michael Howlett, eds., *The Provincial State in Canada: Politics in the Provinces and Territories* (Peterborough, ON: Broadview Press, 2001), 241–75; John Richards and Larry Pratt, *Prairie Capitalism: Power and Influence in the New West* (Toronto: McClelland and Stewart, 1979), chs. 5–6.
14. For a critical examination of this trend, see John Shields and B. Mitchell Evans, *Shrinking the State: Globalization and Public Service "Reform"* (Halifax: Fern-

Taxation as an Expression of Community / 43

wood Publishing, 1998), esp. ch.4.
15. *Report...*, 5.
16. Ibid., 4.
17. Ibid., 9.
18. Ibid., 9.
19. Ibid., 10.
20. For an insightful account of the role the idea of a trade-off in contemporary political debate, see Macpherson, "Liberalism as Trade-offs," in *The Rise and Fall of Economic Justice and Other Essays* (Oxford and New York: Oxford University Press, 1985), 44–54.
21. For a brilliant and powerful critique of this assumption, see Tibor Scitovsky, *The Joyless Economy: An Inquiry into Human Satisfaction and Consumer Dissatisfaction* (Oxford: Oxford University Press, 1976).
22. Charles E. Lindblom, *Politics and Markets: The World's Political-Economic Systems* (New York: Basic Books, 1977), 173.
23. Ibid., 172. Lindblom was concerned about the implications this had for liberal democracy, because these "public functions" were carried out without public control through elected governments.
24. Ibid., 11. Emphasis added.
25. Ibid., 13.
26. Ibid., 13. Emphasis added.
27. Ibid., 6.
28. Ibid., 5.
29. Ibid., 14.
30. Ibid., 14–15. Emphasis added.
31. Like its federal counterpart, the Commission was strongly influenced by Henry Simon. As noted above, Simon argued on behalf of a progressive tax structure based on a comprehensive interpretation of taxable income, which included both consumption and savings. He believed, in other words, that increases in the market value of assets, and not just spending on goods and services, should be fully subject to taxation. Inasmuch as the current system provides significant deductions and exemptions for personal savings and capital, the "income" tax has in effect become a consumption tax. Because lower income people consume more of their income than higher income individuals, the progressive nature of the tax structure is thereby diminished.
32. *Report...*, 10.
33. Ibid., 14.
34. Ibid., 14.
35. Ibid., 14.
36. Ibid., 14.
37. Ibid., 15.
38. Ibid., 10.
39. Ibid., 13.
40. Ibid., 40. The emphasis is in the original.
41. Ibid., 211. Emphasis added.
42. See the highly interesting series of tables on various facets of the provincial economy and government budgets beginning on 42 of the *Report...*.
43. *Report...*, 156.
44. Ibid., 157. Emphasis added. (The *Report* ... did indicate that during the course

of its hearings some concern had been expressed about the tax policies of the federal government.) Elsewhere in the *Report...*, the Commission noted that factors shaping income in the province "lie largely outside the control of governments in this province and in the realm of national policies and international events. The government of the province may by certain of its policies exercise some moderating influence upon these effective forces. But even with a limited objective in view, we doubt that operations in the field of tax policy as such will have much to offer in comparison with other policy fields which provide the government with opportunities for positive action" (13)

45. Ibid., 157–8. Emphasis added. Interestingly, the Commission argues that effective economic "control" could only in all likelihood be achieved through the use of fiscal policy, rather than monetary policy, which was "at present guided largely by the vital needs of exchange rate stability and the international money market. Because of this orientation, it is to be doubted that they can readily be used effectively in the pursuit of purely domestic policies." (158) This is precisely the reverse of policy 'wisdom' today.

46. The primary change was from a system of tax rental, under which primarily the federal government levied personal and corporate income taxes, to one of tax sharing and tax collection, under which both federal and provincial governments levied these taxes, with the federal government collecting on behalf of both. For a detailed and valuable discussion of this shift in the context of the history of federal-provincial relations, see David B. Perry, *Financing the Canadian Federation, 1867 to 1995: Setting the Stage for Change* (Toronto: Canadian Tax Foundation, 1997), chs.3–5.

47. *Report...* 209. The Commission held that the "apparent balkanization of fiscal activities as illustrated by such evidence as [the steadily increasing share of revenues going to provincial governments and consequent decline in the position of the federal government] and by the fact of the abandonment of the tax rental agreement system, is something to be viewed with concern" (158).

48. *Report...* 156–7.

49. Ibid., 13.

Chapter Three

Taxation as a Barrier to Wellbeing:
Final Report of the Saskatchewan Personal Income Tax Review Committee (1999)

In the decades following the work of the McLeod Commission, much changed economically in Canada and the world. A deep recession in 1974–75, the worst economic downturn since the Great Depression of the 1930s, brought the post-war economic boom to a close and the Keynesian welfare state into crisis. A combination of stagnation and inflation—stagflation—emerged and inaugurated a quarter century of significantly changed economic conditions. Instability has become the hallmark of this era, manifesting itself in, among other things, substantially and persistently higher levels of unemployment, frequently wrenching industrial restructuring and periodic financial crises. Such developments were, and continue to be, exacerbated by economic globalization, the rapid and pervasive movement of goods, services and capital around the world.

In the face of these momentous changes, the dominant Keynesian strategy of government economic management was discredited, its policy tools used to stabilize growth and employment apparently unable to deal with the new situation. It was replaced by a resurgent free market paradigm promoting a diminished role for governments and a significantly enhanced one for competitive markets driven by owners of private wealth in search of ever-expanding profits. Proponents claimed that freeing market forces allegedly bottled up during the heyday of the Keynesian welfare state would generate innovation, wealth creation and renewed economic growth. This argument became the basis of neo-liberalism and its commitments to privatization, deregulation—and tax cutting.

Such developments provided the backdrop against which the government of Saskatchewan created the Saskatchewan Personal Income Tax Review Committee in early 1999. Aside from the changes that had occurred in the world and Canadian economies, there had also emerged a series of perceived provincial concerns to which the government felt compelled to respond; the creation of the Review Committee was part of its response.

One concern related to Saskatchewan's place in the national economy. In the almost four decades after the McLeod Commission, Saskatchewan had at times enjoyed periods of substantial economic expansion, largely under the impact of major resource developments and high world prices for products such as oil, gas, potash and uranium, as well as, on occasion, agricultural commodities. Still, overall, Saskatchewan's position nationally had not changed dramatically from what it had been in the mid-1960s, when the Royal Commission submitted its report: it still enjoyed *per capita* income levels slightly below the national average.[1] Consequently, the quest for stable and steady economic development continued to daunt policymakers. The tasks seemed all the more challenging in the face of much more dynamic and vigorous growth in neighbouring Alberta, which many in business and government alike came to view as the economic model to be emulated.

Adding to the challenges were economic concerns, both cyclical or short-term and secular or long-term, notably the ongoing crisis in agriculture as reflected both in the recent precipitous decline in producer incomes, particularly for those producing grains, and in the continuing, longer term tendency for smaller farms to disappear and those remaining to become larger and more capital intensive. Total net farm income declined from $1.359 billion in 1996 to $422 million in 2000.[2] With respect to the number and size of farms, in 1941 there were 138,713 farms averaging 432 acres; by 1996, there were only 56,995 farms, whose average size was 1152 acres. With respect to the amount of capital—livestock and poultry, land and buildings, machinery and implements—in 1956, for example, the average value per farm was $22,384, while by 1996 this figure had reached $525,916.[3]

While the Royal Commission had been correct in projecting a declining role for agriculture in the provincial economy—mineral production, primarily oil and gas, potash, uranium and coal, has supplanted it—the crisis had, and continues to have, a dampening effect on provincial economic activity, especially in light of weakening prices internationally for some of these other primary resources (notably potash and uranium; oil and gas have fared better). As well, the social and cultural significance of agricultural production in a province that takes considerable pride in its agrarian and rural heritage has made the crisis more visible, painful and controversial than GDP figures alone would indicate. Historically, agrarian producers and organized farm movements were vital components of Saskatchewan's social structure as the province evolved following its creation in 1905. They were the driving force behind the establishment of the Saskatchewan Wheat Pool and the cooperative movement generally, as well as the formation during the Depression of the CCF. They also shaped the political culture, that is, the character of dominant political values, in a strongly populist direction. Although the number of agrarian producers has dramatically declined and agriculture's share of the provincial economy has diminished, by Canadian standards it continues to play a relatively significant role.[4]

In short, agrarian producers have had a central place in the construction in Saskatchewan of civil society: "a sphere of social interaction between economy and state, composed above all of the intimate sphere (especially the family), the sphere of associations (especially voluntary associations), social movements, and forms of public communication ... created through forms of self-constitution and self-mobilization."⁵ In this light, ideas about the individual and society can persist even if the original conditions that gave rise to them change. They continue to be carried, in varying degrees, by the institutions that are the legacy of a society's formative influences.⁶

There were two other developments in Saskatchewan which signaled the move from the era of the Keynesian welfare state to that of neo-liberalism. One of these related to the changing character of the governing party, the New Democratic Party. The NDP was the inheritor of the legacy of the CCF, which had built the welfare state in Saskatchewan and had established the Royal Commission on Taxation. Echoing the change that occurred with the federal CCF after 1961, the Saskatchewan party adopted the NDP label after 1964, when it lost power to the Liberal Party. Returning to office in 1971, the provincial NDP under Allen Blakeney adopted an activist, "province-building" stance that featured significant public investment in resource development, notably in potash, oil and gas, and uranium, coupled with some enhancement of the social safety net and expansion of public infrastructure. This was an "entrepreneurial" government committed to public investment in wealth creating activities, primarily in the resource sector, and hence to the values of a social democracy linked to extensive state economic activity and planning.⁷

Interestingly, the NDP government pursued much of this agenda after the 1974–75 recession and the momentous changes that followed in its wake. The emergence of more conservative ideas and political movements in the late 1970s did not initially threaten the position of the government or its policy agenda. In a way, the argument of the McLeod Commission that the people of Saskatchewan harboured a strong commitment to a major economic role for government and a high level of public services seemed vindicated by the success of a social democratic party and government in the new, post-Keynesian era.⁸

However, in the wake of another major recession, the NDP did lose power in 1982 to a Progressive Conservative party armed with a strong ideological commitment to the market and the private sector. The new government, under Grant Devine, embraced what in the early nineteen eighties came to be known as a New Right agenda: the diminution of the role of government, coupled with the promotion of an aggressively competitive individualism that emphasized self-reliance shaped by patriarchal and Christian values. During its tenure in office, the government generated enormous controversy over its ideological position and many of its policies. But it succeeded in introducing into political debate in the province conservative views that had not before figured so prominently.

At the same time, it pursued its own, private sector driven, but state supported, "province building" strategies. This involved the use of joint ventures, loan guarantees, subsidies and tax concessions to foster a range of economic endeavours, such as a heavy oil upgrader, a privately owned fertilizer plant, a computerized translation service and a shopping cart manufacturing plant. In addition it privatized, or sold off to the private sector, a number of government owned enterprises, most notably Saskoil and the Saskatchewan Mining Development Corporation. The success of these policies was mixed at best; one consequence of them was a significantly increased level of government debt.[9]

At the time the NDP returned to office in 1991 (where it remains, although since 1999 only with the support originally of three, later two, members of the provincial legislature who had been elected as Liberals), powerful forces within the ranks of business and government in Canada were vigorously promoting the idea that the country faced a debt crisis.[10] Profligate governments had over the course of the previous two decades, it was claimed, spent wantonly and recklessly, thereby threatening financial ruin. The only cure lay in dramatically reducing state expenditures, raising taxes (temporarily) and in general radically cutting the size of government. Governments across the country of all political stripes came to embrace the alleged need to eliminate budget deficits and shrink the overall size of public debt.[11]

The Saskatchewan NDP was not immune to this pressure or indeed to the general shift of political debate to the right, particularly in the wake of the years of Conservative government. In particular, the new government readily accepted the argument that Saskatchewan faced a "debt wall." This is the idea, again parallel to the "common sense" assumption that governments could "go broke," that in the face of dangerously "high" debt levels, the capacity of governments to take on debt had been reached. As a result, international lenders might "foreclose" on a political jurisdiction, or in the extreme case, might even refuse to purchase government bonds and demand immediate payment of outstanding debt. But primarily lenders would punish governments for their alleged fiscal mismanagement by downgrading the value of their bonds and therefore imposing higher interest rates to take into account the supposedly greater risks to investors. The NDP believed that as a result of the ostensibly wasteful legacy of its predecessor, it had to take painful but necessary restraint measures to restore the province to fiscal health.

Hence, while nominally social democratic, the new government largely forsook the "entrepreneurial" practices of previous NDP ministries. Furthermore, since its initial election in 1991, the NDP has pursued a stringent fiscal conservatism founded on its unwavering commitments to yearly balanced budgets and debt reduction. The province has long depended for economic growth on both government investments in income generating activities and government expenditures for goods and services, privately and publicly produced (including social services). Hence, this commitment to traditional financial orthodoxy has had an impact on economic activity, one that the government has appeared willing to accept.¹² At the same time, the government has virtually abandoned the idea that the public sector can and should lead the way or at least play a vital role in promoting wellbeing. It now prefers to rely almost exclusively on the private sector to undertake the necessary commitments, while facilitating market-driven activity "by making major investments in education, transportation and technology" and "by giving people the tools to succeed in a growing, diversified economy."¹³ And, one should add, by tax cuts.¹⁴

The other development that indicated the move from Keynesianism to neo-liberalism was the practice of successive federal governments, since the 1980s, of pursuing their own agendas of fiscal restraint in response to the supposed deficit and debt crises. Among other things, this involved cuts to federal fiscal transfers in support of programs under provincial jurisdiction, transfers upon which Saskatchewan has historically relied.¹⁵ It also involved something else. As noted before, during the Keynesian era the federal government had used its tax and spending policies in part to manage the economy by smoothing out the cycles of boom and bust, of inflation and deflation, to which a capitalist system is prone. In other words, public sector budgets performed a stabilization function, one that governments still aware of the impact of the Great Depression and the demands of wartime finance seemed willing to assume.¹⁶ By the 1990s, however, the federal government had committed itself to the neo-liberal strategy of freeing up market forces and in effect abandoned stabilization policy and the rationale formerly used to support it. Tax policy was thus disconnected from questions of economic management and viewed instead from the perspective of its consequences for the government's budgetary position (i.e., whether the government was running a deficit or surplus) and its effects on individual incentives to produce, that is, whether or not existing taxes encouraged people to work and invest. By the late 1990s, the federal government began to enjoy large budget surpluses and, at the same time, became increasingly sensitive to demands for tax reductions, ostensibly to make the Canadian economy more productive and competitive. It therefore substantially cut personal income taxes. This in turn reduced provincial tax revenues, which since 1962, have been calculated as a percentage of basic federal tax. As a result, provinces began casting about for alternative fiscal arrangements that would more fully insulate them from the consequences of federal initiatives, while providing them leeway to pursue their own economic strategies.

In 1998, the federal government recognized the decentralizing implications of this situation and indicated its willingness to allow the provinces to levy personal income taxes directly on income, instead of applying their rates to the basic federal tax. No longer would provincial tax revenues be tied directly to federal ones, although the federal government would continue to set the tax base and collect taxes on behalf of the provinces (Quebec excepted). In 1999, Alberta became the first province to announce its intention to move to a tax on income. It did so beginning in 2001; the other provinces, including Saskatchewan, have either followed suit or are planning to do so.[17]

The federal-provincial fiscal arrangements in place in the early 1960s and the assumptions supporting them helped sustain the value commitments inherent in the McLeod Commission. The logic of the contemporary arrangements suggests a rather different conception of the place and role of the tax system. The move from a system of "tax on tax" to one of a "tax on income" severs the last substantial link with the unified system of fiscal policy and management put in place during the Second World War and post-war eras. That system provided the federal government with the means to fund national programs in areas of provincial jurisdiction and to pursue policies of fiscal stabilization, along with some measure of income redistribution. While funding of provincial programs continues, albeit diminished, the "self-regulating" market, which supposedly if left to itself will correct any imbalances and is thus self-stabilizing, is now seen as the only truly appropriate vehicle for ensuring both continuing growth and the most appropriate distribution of income and wealth. There is still room for public goods not delivered by the private sector and for modest amelioration of the economic inequalities inherent in a capitalist market system, but overall, the idea, central to the Keynesian era, that the state had a directing role to play in the economy has been set aside.[18]

With the economic role of the state de-emphasized and government seen as having at best a limited ability to ensure material wellbeing, people are more likely to view taxation a hardship. With its commitment to reduced government, neo-liberalism offers intellectual and ideological support for the conception that taxes are inherently a burden. In Canada, the primary carrier of neo-liberal ideas, the business community, has been vocal in promoting the necessity for substantial tax reductions, and governments, federal and provincial, have heard its voice. The Canadian Council of Chief Executives (formerly the Business Council on National Issues), which represents the biggest companies in Canada, and think-tanks, such as the Fraser and C.D. Howe institutes, present the issue as among the most pressing to the overwhelming majority of Canadians. There is little evidence such is the case; however there does appear to be support for tax "relief" among middle- and working-class people.[19] The idea that taxes are burdensome has been reinforced by the shift on the part of federal and provincial governments over the last two decades toward an increasing reliance for revenue on personal income tax, which falls relatively more heavily on wage and salary earners, and away from corporate income taxation, thereby lessening the impact on the wealthy.[20] But it also reflects another dimension of the economic instability of the last quarter century: stagnating real incomes for individuals and increased hours of work, coupled with reductions in public programs and tax/transfer benefits.[21] Under these circumstances, taxes will seem more onerous. Thus, the "taxation" problem may in fact be an "income" problem.

All of these elements set the context for the work of the Saskatchewan Personal Income Tax Review Committee. In the wake of the federal-provincial agreement to change the tax collection arrangements, the Committee was charged primarily with the task of examining whether the province should itself move to a system of tax on income. Its final report did in fact recommend such a move. But it also did something more fundamental. It offered a rationale for a more individualist and less communal understanding of citizenship and the relation of the state to the economy. In doing so, the Committee reflected not only what might be called the macro-ideological climate of neo-liberalism, it also drew upon, if for the most part implicitly, a currently influential account of human motivation: rational choice.

Rational choice, also called public or social choice when applied to political institutions making collective decisions, has a long history. Its roots lie to a considerable extent in the political theory of the great seventeenth-century English philosopher, Thomas Hobbes, who argued that society was composed of self-contained individuals engaged in a constant struggle for power. Its main vehicle is neo-classical economics, and in particular microeconomics, the theory of markets and prices. Neo-classical economics has grown up along with the development, spread and deepening of capitalist market relations and has served both to explain and justify the system. At its core is the idea that free individuals are driven by the pursuit of self-interest and that all individual actions involve fulfilling to the greatest extent possible individual preferences. This is tied to the realization of some individual good, the core of wellbeing. The maximization of wellbeing, or utility, is ultimately what all individuals seek; it defines their humanity. (Hence, it is often associated with the philosophical doctrine known as utilitarianism, although by no means would all utilitarians see themselves as proponents of a radically individualist account of rational choice.) Rational individuals choose those courses of action, the means, that most efficiently and thus effectively fulfill their objectives, or ends. In effect, people are cost-benefit calculators, who seek either to maximize their benefits given a certain level of resources or minimize the costs of achieving their goals. Ultimately, in the words of one rational-choice, or public-choice, theorist, "[t]he basic behavioral postulate of public choice, as for economics, is that man is an egoistic, rational, utility maximizer."[22]

Those who embrace rational choice tend to prefer and promote free markets and private enterprise, because they see the market as founded upon, and as giving the fullest opportunity for, free, individual choice. They see this as a matter of both rationality and morality: Interference with free, or rational, choice through, for example, state intervention in the marketplace, always threatens to distort individual calculations of wellbeing, and thus undermine rationality. But it also undermines morality in that it threatens both the right of individuals to make their own choices according to their own understanding of their interests and also, under certain circumstances, the need for people to face the consequences of their actions (what economists call "moral hazard"). At the same time, state institutions are seen as bodies of self-interested individuals who will always seek to use political authority to their own advantage, at the expense of others (consumers, entrepreneurs, workers, taxpayers); on the other hand, those who call upon the state for support for their activities are deemed "special interest groups." Likewise, they seek to use state power for their own, selfish purposes and against the public interest, which is identified with free, individual choices in the pursuit of the competitive maximization of utility.

Ultimately, rational- or public-choice theorists hold that the results of free market competition are "neutral" in that they reflect the success of maximizing agents in fulfilling their purposes, satisfying their wants and, through their choices, exercising their capacities. By contrast, state activities, including taxation, are compulsory, non-neutral, even unnatural limits on free choice that are the products of the exercise of power and authority, which are always suspect and in need of justification.

While the theory of rational choice has in one form or another been around a long time, its recent (re)emergence has clearly gone hand in hand with the resurgence of free market ideas more generally. But its success can also be attributed to the failure of official Keynesianism (if not Keynes, himself) to develop an alternative account of the individual, one that is more in tune with its more positive conception of politics and political institutions.

The "crisis" of Keynesianism that took shape in the 1970s raised the question of the so-called micro-foundations of both economic theory and practice: the nature of the individual as an economic agent and the structure of markets and prices, that is, the institution within which individuals engaged in economic activity and the "cues" they used to determine where to put their resources. In practice, Keynesian policies tended to be macro-economic, that is, concerned with levels of output, employment and prices in the economy as a whole and how to ensure continuing high growth and full employment.[23] When these policies seemed to fail, conservative, free market economists in particular claimed this was because such policies flew in the face of what people were actually like and what they really wanted. What individuals were like was utility maximizing, self-interested rational agents—that is, rational choosers. What they wanted was the opportunity to freely pursue their goals by determining where to put their resources. Only free markets unencumbered by government regulation could accomplish this—only free markets were attuned to human nature.

This is why, under the influence of neo-liberalism, governments have pursued policies of deregulation of markets, privatization of government agencies, companies and services, and tax reductions. These are microeconomic policies. In effect, they reflect the position that all economics is micro; the macro world of output and employment, of so-called economic aggregates of consumption, savings and investment, takes care of itself, as long as individuals are "free to choose."[24] Free marketers rejected the Keynesian idea that on its own the market could not generate appropriate levels of economic activity or maintain stable growth without wrenching cycles of boom and bust and the hardship these brought. In short, they rejected the view that markets could much of the time fail: pure market failure was a marginal phenomenon. Left to itself, it was claimed, a market economy tended to equilibrium: individual markets would clear in that supply and demand, for goods, services, labour and capital, would be brought into balance through the "natural" forces of competition. And, as indicated above, all this would be based on free, rational individual choices made by people who knew what they wanted better than anyone else did and, in so choosing, determined their own fate. At the level of the economy and society as a whole, the outcome would be both efficient and just.[25]

Given that proponents of rational choice claim it to be universally true, it would seem that they might have difficulty explaining how it could work at all during the period of rapid, post-war growth, when Keynesianism was in full flower. At the very least, there must have been something about Keynesian policies that accorded with the self-interest of large numbers of people. If this were so, then even assuming people are primarily if not exclusively self-interested, the very notions of "self" and "interest" are richer in meaning and significance than the received theory of self-interest suggests.[26] In effect, Keynesianism may be said to have relied upon an insufficiently articulated conception of the individual—a different microfoundation, a more "social" individual—that at the same time its own policies might have also helped create or at least bring to light. Of course, the rational-choice view, never really challenged during the heyday of the Keynesian welfare state (except by thinkers and actors more radical than were most Keynesians), is visibly out there now, and was then, if less obtrusively. It currently seems to be overwhelmingly dominant. But it may be that we have multiple "selves," a point to which I will return in Chapter Five.

A neo-liberal defender of rational choice might well reply that what really happened in the Keynesian era was that those "special interest groups" identified earlier, particularly trade unions but also other equality seeking groups (women, ethnic and racial minorities), got hold of the state and used political power to serve their own interests at the expense of others, who formed the "public" and whose primary interest was in supposedly free competition. The market account of human nature had not been transcended, just suppressed. And even if it could be shown that more than just narrowly self-interested groups supported the welfare state, and benefitted from it, that a majority of the public did so and voted for welfare state policies at the ballot box, this would prove only that democracy itself was seriously, if not fatally, flawed. (As will be discussed below, there are those who historically have made this case and make it now.)

This is not the place to pursue these matters further; obviously much more could be said about rational choice and its contemporary role. But quite apart from the specific issues raised by debates about micro-foundations, what these debates indicate is that the clash of perspectives and theories in economics or political economy necessarily carries with it implications about what people are, or should be, like, and what society is, or should be.

What is important in the context of the kind of tax study considered in this chapter is that the use of rational-choice analysis and themes leaves a distinctive imprint on the style and texture, the analysis and the arguments, of such a study. As noted above, it claims to be a universal theory of human motivation and behaviour, true of individuals at all times and in all places. The rational "chooser" is the same in Regina or Riyadh. Questions about history and institutions, except insofar as these might say something about choice, have little place. There is as a result a kind of "bloodlessness" to the account. This is not a matter merely of aesthetic preference but of intellectual penetration and insight. It has consequences for the way in which the issues raised, and even society itself, are understood, explained and evaluated.

In fulfillment of its primary task, the Personal Income Tax Review Committee, which was headed by Jack Vicq, an accountant who, interestingly, had served as a researcher for the McLeod Commission, was asked to consider four objectives: fairness in the tax system; support for the family; simplicity for the taxpayer and government; and competitiveness in attracting jobs and investment. The commitments to support for the family and competitiveness immediately stand out. The Royal Commission made no such reference to family support. No doubt, this reflected the fact that, at the time, the single, male breadwinner model of the family was widely taken for granted and viewed as stable. However, it is at least plausible that "support for families" has become a mantra in the current era when direct public provisioning is increasingly de-emphasized and private provisioning is encouraged, and even celebrated—with the family as a critical element in this. The irony is that the "family" is now singled out in this way precisely as real families have become more variegated and complex.[27]

The theme of competitiveness explicitly flies in the face of the position staked out by the Royal Commission: taxation policy as such has little effect on investment decisions. "Competitiveness" implies that fiscal policy must be about providing conditions under which the private sector can flourish—and that alone. This is at odds with the view that economic wellbeing is necessarily a complex process of private and public provisioning, that in principle there is nothing to distinguish a dollar of public from a dollar of private expenditure. Both might be said to involve "public choice": one exercised individually through private market exchanges, the other collectively via the state. While the emphasis on competitiveness could well acknowledge both forms of choice, it is clear that in this case they are not equal: the latter must serve the former, be the private choices those of individuals or of families.

Making private resources available to individuals considered as market actors is the assumption behind the primary claim the Committee makes: personal income tax rates are too high and must be brought down in a new provincial system that would tax income directly. To be sure, the "majority of people from whom the Committee heard supported a progressive tax system—a system whereby those who earn more pay a higher proportion of their income as tax."[28] Nonetheless, just as the context for the McLeod Commission was the work of the federal Carter Commission and similar bodies in other provinces, so the context for the Review Committee was the establishment by several provinces of committees exploring ways to lower taxes. In addition to this, as noted earlier, Alberta and Ontario had undertaken highly publicized tax cutting initiatives. "Tax competitiveness" had become the order of the day.

Thus the Committee devoted a substantial portion of its Final Report to comparisons between levels of personal income taxation in Saskatchewan and other jurisdictions with which the province allegedly competes for investment and employment.[29] On the basis of its figures, the Committee claimed that Saskatchewan citizens paid significantly higher taxes than did residents of Ontario and other Western provinces. The Committee held that high personal taxes were major factors in the decisions of youth and those in the twenty-five to forty-nine age group to seek opportunity elsewhere. In particular, existing marginal tax rates—that is, the rates paid on the last dollar of taxable income—posed disincentives for skilled workers and middle- and high-income earners.[30]

Recall that the McLeod Commission argued that comparing different tax rates among jurisdictions by itself provided an inadequate basis for assessing tax burdens. If tax "costs" were to be accurately gauged, it was necessary to relate taxes to the benefits received from them. Other than comparative tax tables, the Committee provided little evidence in support of its contention that high taxes posed disincentives. But even more interesting is what this line of analysis assumes. The Committee's approach to the question of marginal tax rates implies a rational-choice view of individuals, their motives and purposes: As rational beings, people calculate utility in an ongoing way. High marginal rates of taxation dampen productive activity and induce individuals to invest their energies more profitably outside the high tax jurisdiction. The Committee clearly drew here on the ideas of neo-classical economists, who since the 1970s have argued that high marginal tax rates reduce productivity and hence economic growth.³¹ But the Committee itself tells us little about exactly how individuals might calculate wellbeing, or even identify it.

In any case, the Committee suggested that while high marginal rates affect all those who pay the highest rate of slightly over fifty percent (i.e., those earning in excess of $62,200, according to the figures cited in the report), the most significant effect was on those 5600 taxpayers with taxable incomes in excess of $100,000. The Committee referred to a study prepared by the Saskatchewan Chamber of Commerce, which claimed that a "significant number" of Saskatchewan business owners (i.e., high income earners) were arranging their finances so that they would pay taxes in Alberta and avoid Saskatchewan's "high" marginal rates.³²

According to the Committee, these high-income earners, who represent less than 2 percent of Saskatchewan tax filers, pay almost 18 percent of personal income taxes. The Final Report did not indicate what percentage of provincial *income* this group earns. But even without such information, the existing arrangement would on the face of it conform to the requirements of a progressive tax system, for which the Committee detected widespread public support. Nevertheless, the Committee argued that the marginal tax rates paid by the highest income earners made the province's personal rates uncompetitive. These needed to be lowered if such individuals were to be discouraged from becoming tax migrants. By implication, the Committee accepted as unproblematic, if not unavoidably necessary, the way in which income is distributed through market relations among individuals, groups and classes. In other words, there was no specific issue of what political theorists and philosophers call "distributive justice," that is, the question of how resources are to be shared among people living together in a society.³³ In essence, there was no issue of political morality or value here, no normative question.

But if the alleged need for tax competitiveness posed no normative challenge, the question of "support for the family" was avowedly treated as a normative matter. The Commission claimed that the current system, in which a single-income family paid significantly more tax than a dual-income family earning the same amount, was unfair. The Final Report took this position even though it claimed that taxation should be based on the individual. Individual taxation "allows the income tax system to avoid creating a disincentive to labour force participation by the spouse."³⁴ In the circumstances, it would be the female spouse who would most likely be discouraged from labour force participation in a different system of taxation.

In effect, "one-income family" is a surrogate for the old male-breadwinner model. This is reinforced by the Committee's views about tax deductions for childcare expenses. The Committee appeared to accept the claim, currently made in certain conservative circles, that the existing federal provisions for deducting childcare expenditures are inequitable.³⁵ Specifically, it noted that this deduction is claimed by two-income families (presumably because they purchase childcare services) but is generally denied to one-income families (where presumably a spouse undertakes the care-giving without direct payment). In addition, it pointed out that the province provides for lower income families a tax deduction in support of dependent children. According to the Committee, "the tax system should recognize the additional costs associated with raising children for all families."[36]

What makes this issue so interesting is that it represents a deviation from the logic of rational choice otherwise evident throughout the report. Apparently, there *are* groups—families—that should be recognized as such in a tax system otherwise based on the individual. The tax system must acknowledge all childcare providers, including stay-at-home ones who, given the usual domestic division of labour, would almost certainly be female. The rationally choosing individual not only might be said to reflect male values but *is* male.

The combination of tax competitiveness and support for the family as goals of tax reform led the Committee to recommend that the largest tax savings go to one-income families with children. Indeed under the Committee's proposal for lower provincial marginal rates, a single-income family earning $75,000 per year would see its personal income taxes reduced from $11,128 in 1999 to $7,744 by 2003.[37] This move represents a significant shift not only in fiscal policy but also in social policy. It goes beyond the Committee's stated commitment to treat families in equal circumstances "equally." As noted above, the Committee even compromised its position on individual "free" choice and a system based on individual earnings to justify its recommendations on family taxation.[38]

Just as the Committee's perspectives on tax competitiveness and support for families reflected significant changes from an earlier era in the perceived role of taxation and the nature of community, so too did its account of tax fairness. At the core of its account is the issue of progressive taxation. It is instructive to note some subtle but important differences here between the logic of the Royal Commission report and the Review Committee's approach.

As already indicated, the Committee detected significant support for a system of progressive taxation. According to the Final Report, "Saskatchewan's current personal tax system is one of the most progressive tax structures in Canada, as almost 80 percent of taxes paid by the average Saskatchewan family resulted from the personal income tax."[39] This was noticeably higher than comparable figures in Ontario and the other Western provinces. From the perspective of the Committee, such differences raised the question whether the system was *too* progressive, whether fairness in pursuit of equality had gone too far.

This focus reflected a dramatically different conception of fairness from that advanced by the tax studies of the Keynesian era. The pursuit of fairness then clearly involved some measure of egalitarian redistribution. To be sure, the Royal Commission challenged the view that only the personal income tax was truly "fair." Nonetheless, it held that existing tax rates were not confiscatory—and at the time marginal rates of taxation were much more steeply graduated than they are currently.[40]

The Personal Income Tax Review Committee saw the matter differently. Not only were marginal rates too high, but also the province had become too reliant on the personal income tax for revenue.[41] The Committee thus called for a new system of significantly flatter tax rates. (A flat tax rate, such as that put in place in Alberta, sets one rate for all income above a certain threshold, as opposed to a graduated system of rates applied to increasing levels of income.) The result would see personal income taxes reduced by $430 million by the 2003–4 tax year.[42]

To at least partially offset the loss of revenue involved, the Committee recommended a shift to allegedly under-utilized revenue sources. Primarily, it proposed that the current 6 percent provincial sales tax be reduced to 5 percent and applied to a significantly broader consumption base. Under its proposal, only food, shelter, prescription drugs and reading materials would be fully exempt from the tax.

Consumption taxes such as sales taxes tend to be regressive. Because a sales tax is applied at a fixed rate on all purchases, it takes a larger portion of income from lower income people, who in any event tend to spend virtually all their income on goods and services for consumption. The Final Report acknowledged this and hence recommended "offsets." These would be delivered through existing income support programs and would reduce the effects of an expanded sales tax on low-income individuals. The Committee viewed this as particularly important, because it claimed its new rate structure, in conjunction with significantly enhanced tax credits that would apply to lower incomes, would remove over 58,000 low-income earners from the income tax rolls.[43]

So in spite of its emphasis on individual economic incentives, the Review Committee did not totally disregard questions of income distribution in its analysis. Yet it accepted the current conventional wisdom that taxation should not significantly modify market-generated inequalities. The tax system had to promote efficiency in the mobilization of resources, which can only come about if people have the incentive of higher returns for their efforts, over equity or equality. What this implies is that the range of public goods, or goods provided collectively through governments and financed substantially by taxes, should be devoted primarily to securing those conditions that make possible the private economic activities of families, individuals and businesses. Such goods would include security for persons and property, education and, presumably, healthcare, inasmuch as this can be seen as ensuring that people can be productive. On this view, great caution should be exercised in providing public goods that were more explicitly or avowedly redistributive. These would include programs of income support or assistance, funded by progressive taxes, which might match or even exceed wages paid for work in the private sector.

But in another sense, this position involves the idea that progressive taxation (if not in fact taxation *per se*) is in itself redistributive just because, broadly speaking, it "takes" resources from people who have acquired them in the private sector for use in support of purposes defined by governments. In a formal political democracy, governments are popularly elected. Therefore, individuals who have not been able to match those who are most successful in their economic lives—in an unequal capitalist society, the unsuccessful are the majority—select those who do the "taking." The people selected to govern determine the use of these resources on behalf of the people who chose them. Of course, dissatisfaction with existing representative democratic institutions is triggered by the sense that elected representatives do *not* act on behalf of those who have chosen them. Indeed, the deep concern about the role of money in politics is based on the fear that elected legislators represent those who have the wealth to contribute to election campaigns—the economically successful—and not the voters at large. Nonetheless the basic point remains. *Because it addresses issues of significance for all, the act of governing is itself "redistributive." Indeed, since government acts on behalf of the society as a whole, the very idea of a social body is inherently redistributive, a modification of market outcomes*. This is why defenders of market freedoms, of *laissez-faire* and limited government, of rational choice, have historically identified the conflict between "individualism" and "collectivism" as a key problem confronting liberal democracies and have expressed the fear that the latter could swallow up the former.[44] This is also why, in its tone and texture, the Review Committee report seemed to be uncomfortable with progressive taxation, although it never explicitly said so.

This second dimension of the question of taxation and redistribution is important because, even if it could be shown that government expenditures benefit the more affluent as much as, or even more than, the less affluent, this would not do away with opposition to progressive taxation. For what is at stake is exactly the question of how we understand the individual and his or her motives and the nature of the social bond itself. The point to note here is that this now conventional wisdom bumped up against what the Committee acknowledged as widespread support for progressive taxation. Presumably, the arguments of the Final Report would encourage "voters ... and the political leaders they elect, to determine whether the politics of redistribution continue to take priority over the economics of growth."[45]

The Committee's proposed tax reductions were in fact substantially richer than those planned at the time by the provincial government. While the Committee did not address government spending, it did support the government's longstanding commitment to balanced budgets. The implication is that any revenue shortfall would have to be made up either by an even more extensive use of its recommended alternative revenue sources or by reductions in expenditures.[46]

The ability to use budgetary outlays in support of greater equality would be diminished. In any case, neither progressive taxation nor public spending on, for example, job creation or income support is now viewed as a significant policy option. The Review Committee report appeared in accord with this. In effect, its response to the problem of inadequate incomes was the same as its recommendations for high-income earners: tax cuts. With the state reducing its take, lower income individuals would have more available to meet their needs—privately.

Again, there is an implied de-emphasis on a central role for public provisioning. The Royal Commission on Taxation had connected taxation to expenditures. It argued that not only were existing levels of spending, and thus taxation, acceptable, but that it was likely there would be public demand for even higher levels of expenditures. By contrast, save for its support of balanced budgets, the Review Committee treated spending hardly at all. The McLeod Commission assumed general support for spending *and* taxation. The Vicq Committee assumed widespread support for tax cuts above all else. It did not treat the issue of public support for state expenditures. But its position implied that demands for spending, particularly on social programs, were fuelled to a considerable extent by the desire of individuals of modest means to have their needs met through impositions on the more affluent. The failure/unwillingness of the Commission to link taxation with spending, and the necessity for both, suggests at best a grudging acceptance of the role of government in the economy and society.

As indicated above, this has deep roots in the sources of neo-liberal thinking on the economy and the polity. I noted that the Committee acknowledged support for a system of progressive taxation, without elaborating on this point in great detail. But a currently influential argument holds that the Canadian tax system is progressive because, for most taxpayers (i.e., the non-wealthy), the benefits from state spending exceed the costs in taxes paid.[47] The idea here, common to public-choice analysis, is that politicians seeking power "reward" voters by giving the majority what it wants at the expense of the minority, which pays high taxes for benefits it either does not receive or does not need or even want. Whatever might be said about the "costs" versus the "benefits" of state spending, this line of analysis is radically individualist and seems to call into question the notion of community itself. The idea that taxation is not simply a cost borne by self-seeking individuals but an element of citizenship through which they forge common ties with one another finds no place in this account. But then, for such analysts, the polity is just another kind of market.

Views of this sort owe a good deal to free market advocates such as the twentieth century Austrian economists, Friedrich von Hayek and Ludwig von Mises. They questioned the morality of a voting and taxation system that, in their eyes, permitted a majority desiring collective provisioning to saddle an affluent minority with the costs of such programs. (This in effect is a version of the primarily pre-twentieth century argument of the wealthy and powerful that democracy always threatened to become mob rule.) For Hayek and von Mises, people who wanted public expenditures should be prepared to take on the primary responsibility of paying for them. In the words of Hayek: "If a reasonable system of taxation is to be achieved, people must recognize as a principle that the majority which determines what the total amount of taxation should be must also bear it at the maximum rate."[48]

Of course the Final Report nowhere makes reference to scholars such as Hayek or von Mises or their ideas; it is much too brief and its focus much too restricted for that. Nonetheless, it bears the hallmark of this thinking. The most explicit statement of the logic underlying the Review Committee's position makes clear its view of economy and society, of the nature of economic activity and individual motivation:

> The Committee believes a reduction in personal income taxation levels would create a positive economic impact. It would reduce the disincentive effects of high taxation rates on out migration of people to lower rate jurisdictions. It would also have a positive impact on Saskatchewan's consumer and investment climate. *While the consequences of reduced public services would offset these impacts to some extent, we argue that, overall, the impact of lower taxes on public attitudes would be positive.*[49]

Quite apart from whether the specific claims about individual behaviour have been (or can be) substantiated, it is instructive to note the assumptions and commitments involved here. The Final Report assumes an overwhelmingly central place for self-interest and private acquisition, with public motives and purposes barely registering. The effective dismissal of public purposes results in a failure, indeed inability, to examine social, economic and political structures. This renders economic activity and outcomes the product of vaguely defined "public attitudes": the idea that there are structures within which economic activity is undertaken seems curiously absent. This is a "public" of isolated individuals rationally calculating utility, for whom the loss of public services would be more than compensated by the prospects of greater private affluence. Armed with tax cuts and reduced marginal tax rates, such individuals would, as investors and consumers, unleash a wave of entrepreneurial initiatives and generate renewed prosperity. As the fount of fiscal wisdom and the architect of appropriate fiscal policy, John Maynard Keynes has given way. He has been replaced by another Austrian-born economist, Joseph Schumpeter, whose views about the "tax state" we have already noted. Schumpeter was a rival of Keynes, who saw innovative entrepreneurship as the driving force of a capitalist market economy and who viewed extensive state intervention with suspicion. For Schumpeter, capitalism generated waves of "creative destruction." In the constant pursuit of new goods, new methods of production and new forms of productive organization, capitalist enterprise "constantly revolutionizes the economic structure *from within*, incessantly destroying the old one, incessantly creating a new one."[50]

Interestingly, the Final Report cites a 1997 OECD study about the relation of taxation to economic performance. The study claimed it was difficult to determine empirically the effects of taxation on growth. "Taxation may, in fact, be beneficial for the economy if it provides the financial basis for the provision of public goods that improve average living standards and social welfare."[51] This would seem to call into question the idea that reducing personal income tax rates would necessarily spur economic development and is indeed the most significant factor in doing so. Nonetheless, the Committee soldiered on: *"The Committee has concluded that the most persuasive argument for personal income tax reductions are the consequences if nothing is done. Out migration to lower taxed jurisdictions will continue and grow and Saskatchewan's ability to reach the currently forecasted real economic growth will be put at risk."*[52] In view of the position taken in the OECD study, it is unclear why this argument would be "persuasive."

So the Vicq Committee added its voice to those stressing the urgency of personal income tax reductions in the face of perceived threats to economic wellbeing. If the McLeod Commission represented the conventional wisdom of the era of the Keynesian welfare state, the Vicq Committee reflected that of the era of the Schumpeterian workfare state, the era of neoliberalism. There is a shift here from an emphasis on policies which insulate people from the consequences of the operations of the market to policies that more fully expose them to market forces and in particular those of the labour market. The idea is that people need to develop the skills and work discipline that will allow them to be productive participants in a radically changing, internationally competitive, innovation driven market economy. The Schumpeterian workfare state represents "a concern to promote innovation and structural competitiveness in the field of economic policy; and a concern to promote flexibility and competitiveness in the field of social policy.... Thus, while the KWS [Keynesian welfare state] was committed to securing full employment, the SWS [Schumpeterian workfare state] demotes this goal in favour of promoting structural competitiveness. Similarly, while the KWS tried to extend the social rights of its citizens, the SWS is concerned to provide welfare services that benefit business."[53] In effect, individuals are both assumed to be competitive by nature in the pursuit of self-interest and are strongly "encouraged" to actually *be* competitive. Their reward would be higher market returns—hence the need for tax reductions, and especially reduced marginal tax rates, which would permit them to keep more of what they earn. This assumption forms part of the background within which the Personal Income Tax Review Committee did its work.

Yet, there is perhaps an interesting difference in the status of conventional wisdom, then and now. A bit of this emerges in the public response to each examination of the tax system. Both the Royal Commission and the Review Committee held public hearings and entertained submissions from interested groups and individuals. But while there appears to be little evidence in the body of the McLeod Commission report of significant disagreement about the tax system and policy aims and values, this was not the case with the Vicq Committee. As might be expected, business organizations such as the Institute of Chartered Accountants of Saskatchewan and the Saskatoon and Saskatchewan chambers of commerce staunchly supported tax reforms that would reduce rates and the overall income tax "burden."[54] On the other hand, organizations with a different vision of society, such as the Saskatchewan Federation of Labour, the Saskatchewan Action Committee–Status of Women and the Saskatchewan Alternative Budget of Choice took issue with the emphasis on tax cuts, defended "ability to pay" as a principle and in general promoted a continuing and even increased role for government in regulating the market and providing social services.[55] The evidence of disagreement suggests that neo-liberalism may well be dominant but does not enjoy consensus. This may tell us something about the climate of political ideas in a liberal democratic capitalist culture.

Notes

1. A primary measure of the level of economic activity for a jurisdiction is Gross Domestic Product or GDP, roughly the value of all goods and services produced during a given year. In 1965, the year the McLeod Commission report was released, Saskatchewan GDP *per capita* was in current dollars $2,794, while for Canada as a whole the figure was $2,955. The ratio of Saskatchewan GDP *per capita* to that of Canada was 0.95. In 1999, when the Personal Income Tax Review Committee issued its report, the comparable figures were $29,489 versus $31,977. This represented a GDP *per capita* ratio of 0.92. (In 2001, this figure was 0.94). Saskatchewan Bureau of Statistics, *Saskatchewan Provincial Economic Accounts*, May 2002.
2. Saskatchewan Bureau of Statistics, *Economic Review 2001*, Number Fifty Five (December 2001), Table 36.
3. Saskatchewan Agriculture and Food, *Agricultural Statistics 2000* (December 2001), Table 1-3, 1-4.
4. Thus in 2001, agricultural production accounted for approximately 6.3 percent of GDP in Saskatchewan, versus approximately 1.3 percent of GDP for Canada as a whole. These figures were calculated on the basis of data provided in Agriculture and Agri-Food Canada, *Farm Income, Financial Conditions and Government Assistance Data Book* (March 2002), Table C-4; and Saskatchewan Bureau of Statistics, *Saskatchewan Provincial Economic Accounts 2001* (May 2002). The figures can vary with shifts in prices for agricultural products. As the

rapid decline in farm incomes between 1996 and 2000, cited above, attests, prices can fluctuate dramatically (this of course is typically true of resource prices in general, and this is why resource based economies tend to experience dramatic swings in income). Thus in 1996, agricultural production accounted for over 10 percent of GDP. And one could also include in agriculture broadly defined the contributions to GDP made by the agricultural service sector, for example, farm machinery. But this doesn't affect the main point: while less than in the past, agriculture accounts for a relatively significant share of economic activity in Saskatchewan compared to the country as a whole.

5. Jean L. Cohen and Andrew Arato, *Civil Society and Political Theory* (Cambridge MA and London: The MIT Press, 1992), ix. Within political and social theory, there is a debate about the boundaries of the concept of "civil society," that is, what is to be included within it. Some theorists believe, for instance, that civil society includes the capitalist market economy. As my adoption of Cohen and Arato's definition suggests, I believe that the concept is better defined to exclude the economy because, as in Saskatchewan, the idea of a self-organized civil society took root in a context in which popular forces attempted to deal with the compulsive pressures of the market, which appeared to dole out prosperity and misery unfairly and arbitrarily. To be sure, civil society never emerges in a vacuum but exists in a complex and unavoidable relation to both the economy and the state. Economic life under modern capitalism is a central component of social life as a whole, while, as I argue throughout this study, the state forms an indispensable dimension of any social order in that it expresses and helps forge the character of a community.

6. For a discussion of the changing face of rural Saskatchewan in the context of issues relating to civil society and democracy, see Bob Stirling, "Transitions in Rural Saskatchewan," in Howard A. Leeson, ed., *Saskatchewan Politics: Into the Twenty-First Century* (Regina: Canadian Plains Research Center, 2001), 319–36.

7. As was the case with its CCF predecessor, the NDP government did not seek to supplant private capital. The one exception was the nationalization of the potash industry. But even that was undertaken primarily to ensure the province captured locally the returns from the development of an important resource, vital for the manufacture of fertilizer, in which Saskatchewan was the leading world producer. It was not intended to serve as a basis for a wholesale transformation of the Saskatchewan economy in the direction of extensive state ownership beyond the network of crown corporations established by its predecessor and preserved by the Liberal government while it was in office. For an excellent discussion of the economic development strategy of the Blakeney government and some theoretical and policy implications, see David P.M. Gullickson, "Uranium Mining, the State, and Public Policy in Saskatchewan, 1971–1982: The Limits of the Social Democratic Imagination" (unpublished M.A. Thesis, Department of Sociology and Social Studies, University of Regina, 1990).

8. For an account of the strategy and policies of the Blakeney government, see Richards and Pratt, *Prairie Capitalism*....

9. For discussions and assessments of the Progressive Conservatives in power, see James M. Pitsula and Ken Rasmussen, *Privatizing a Province: The New Right in Saskatchewan* (Vancouver: New Star Books, 1990); and Rasmussen, "Saskatch-

ewan: From Entrepreneurial State to Embedded State," 251–2.
10. Workman, *Banking on Deception*.
11. For an excellent account of the "debt crisis" and a critique of the assumptions underlying the claim that it existed, see Harold Chorney, *Sound Finance and Other Delusions: Deficit & Debt Management in the Age of Neo-Liberal Economics* (Working Paper No.4, Department of Political Science, Concordia University, March 1988); and his *The Deficit and Debt Management: An Alternative to Monetarism*, A report by the Canadian Centre for Policy Alternatives, April 1989.
12. This was particularly apparent in one of its earliest budgets (1993), which in the interests of confronting the alleged debt "crisis" featured dramatic tax increases coupled with substantial spending cuts. The government's economic forecasts acknowledged the dampening effects of austerity, in effect justifying "short term pain for long term gain." For a brief assessment of the 1993 budget and its consequences, see Phillip Hansen, "Saskatchewan: The Failure of Political Imagination," *Studies in Political Economy* 43 (Spring 1994), 161–7.
13. Province of Saskatchewan, *Budget Address* (March 30, 2001), 1.
14. For an account of the changing role of the NDP in power in the 1990s and the political setting in which this occurred, see Rasmussen, "Saskatchewan: From Entrepreneurial State to Embedded State," 253ff. Cf. Pitsula and Rasmussen *Privatizing a Province: The New Right in Saskatchewan*. See also Brown, et al., *Saskatchewan Politics From Left to Right '44–99*.
15. Federal fiscal transfers to the province are estimated to represent 21.4 percent of government revenues for Saskatchewan in the 2002–03 budget year; this totals approximately $1.3 billion out of total revenues of $6.1 billion. Especially noteworthy is the size of the equalization payment the federal government provides to provinces with revenue raising capacities below the national average. In Saskatchewan this is estimated to be $530.7 million.
16. Gillespie, *Tax, Borrow & Spend...*100 ff.
17. For an account of recent and prospective changes in tax policies in the context of federal-provincial fiscal arrangements, see Geoffrey Hale, "The Tax on Income and the Growing Decentralization of Canada's Personal Income Tax System," in Harvey Lazar, ed., *Canada: The State of the Federation 1999/2000* (Montreal and Kingston: McGill-Queen's University Press, 2000), 235–62; and Hale, *The Politics of Taxation in Canada*, ch. 12.
18. For a discussion of different economic policy paradigms adopted by governments in North America and Europe, which help put the debate about taxation and the state into context, see Andrew Jackson, "Can There Be a 'Second Wave' in the Third Millennium?" *Studies in Political Economy* 65 (Summer 2001), 39–64.
19. Polling data provided by Environics Research Group indicates that while in a survey undertaken in 1999 77 percent of those surveyed either strongly approved or somewhat approved federal tax cuts (up from 67 percent in 1997; perhaps a sign that the tax cut campaign has had some effect), on a related question about how federal government budget surpluses generated over the course of the late 1990s should be used, a significant plurality, 37 percent, believed they should support additional program spending (versus 25 percent favouring lower taxes, 19 percent supporting debt reduction, and 17 percent supporting some combination of all three). With respect to support for tax cuts,

78 percent of those with 0–8 years of schooling and 80 percent with 9–14 years either strongly or somewhat supported tax cuts, versus 69 percent of those with university degrees. Since levels of education tend to correlate with class location and income level, these figures would suggest support for tax cuts among lower or middle income Canadians, who have seen real incomes decline over the course of the decade of the nineties (see endnote 21).

20. Personal income taxes increased from 10.4 percent of GDP in Canada in 1980 to 14.9 percent in 1996, while corporate income taxes declined from 3.9 percent to 2.7 percent in the same period. Canadian Tax Foundation, *Finances of the Nation 1997*, A3; figures calculated by and cited in Rand Dyck, *Canadian Politics: Critical Approaches* 3rd Edition (Scarborough, ON: Nelson, 2000), 146.

21. The median income for individuals in Canada (the point where one-half of the income earners are above and one-half below the identified figure) was $21,600 in 2000, up from $20,464 in 1997, but still well below the 1990 figure of $23,235 (all figures are adjusted for inflation). Hours of work have also increased significantly over time. See Statistics Canada, *The Daily*, July 7, 2002. See also *The Daily*, August 10, 2001 and "More work—less cash," *The Leader-Post* (Regina), August 11, 2001, A1-2; "Sask. real wages drop seven percent since 1992," *The Leader-Post*, October 21, 2002, B3.

22. Dennis C. Mueller, *Public Choice* (Cambridge: Cambridge University Press, 1979), 1–2. For an application of these ideas to politics and political institutions, see James M. Buchanan, "Politics Without Romance: A Sketch of Positive Public Choice and Its Normative Implications," in Alan Hamlin and Philip Pettit, eds., *Contemporary Political Theory* (New York: Macmillan, 1991), 216–28. For critical treatments of the theory, see Dryzek, *Democracy in Capitalist Times*, ch.5; and Nancy Holmstrom, "Rationality, Solidarity, and Public Goods," in Anatole Anton, Milton Fisk and Nancy Holmstrom, eds., *Not For Sale: In Defense of Public Goods* (Boulder, CO: Westview Press, 2000), 69–88.

Given that the theory of rational choice is central to contemporary, mainstream microeconomic theory, it is not surprising that the most important and influential exponents of it have been academics. Indeed certain universities, such as George Mason University in Virginia, have been strongly identified with the development and spread of the theory.

In this citation, I have deliberately left the term "man" without comment because, as feminist theorists have argued, the idea of rational, egoistic maximization, with its implication that the self stands apart from, and in opposition to, other, equally separate selves, bears the imprint of male-dominated political thinking. For an excellent examination of this and related questions from a feminist perspective, see Marianne A. Ferber and Julie A. Nelson, eds., *Beyond Economic Man: Feminist Theory and Economics* (Chicago and London: The University of Chicago Press, 1993).

23. Of course, governments in the Keynesian era did promote micro-economic policies as well. These included, for example, industrial policies designed to encourage the growth of specific industries and regional development policies designed to encourage more balanced economic growth across a country. For a discussion of such policies in Canada, see Michael Howlett, Alex Netherton, M. Ramesh, *The Political Economy of Canada: An Introduction* second edition (Oxford and New York: Oxford University Press, 1999), ch.11.

24. This was the title of a well-known book by the Nobel Prize winning American

free market economist, Milton Friedman (and his wife, Rose). Friedman has been an important figure in the emergence of neo-liberalism.
25. For an accessible account of the origins of the debate over micro-foundations and its main dimensions, see Meghnad Desai, *Marx's Revenge: The Resurgence of Capitalism and the Death of Statist Socialism* (London and New York: Verso, 2002), ch.16. This work is a sweeping and provocative account of twentieth-century political economy presented against the backdrop of the momentous political, social, economic and cultural events of the century. Desai believes, as did Marx, that the critical question posed by the modern experience is the dynamism of capitalism and its long-term prospects.
26. For a discussion along comparable lines, see Robert Kuttner, *Everything for Sale: The Virtues and Limits of Markets* (Chicago: The University of Chicago Press, 1999), esp. ch.2.
27. Thus what are defined as "traditional" families, that is, married or common law couples with children twenty-four or under living at home, represented 55 percent of all family units in 1981, but only 44 percent in 2001. And within this total, common law family units have jumped from 2.1 percent of all families in 1981 to 7.4 percent in 2001. Statistics Canada, *The Daily*, October 22, 2002.
28. Saskatchewan Personal Income Tax Review Committee, *Final Report and Recommendations* (Regina: Government of Saskatchewan, 1999), 8. (Hereafter referred to as Final Report…) What is left unclear here is the meaning of "higher proportion." A *higher* proportion is not necessarily equivalent to an *increasing* proportion as incomes reach high levels. (In other words, *average* tax rates are not the same as *marginal* tax rates.) Hence, existing federal tax rates, for example, are much flatter than was at one time the case, although they are still considered "progressive."
29. For an analysis which argues that the issue of competitiveness was not necessarily as prominent in the Committee's deliberations as is claimed, see Michael Rushton, "Interprovincial Tax Competition and Tax Reform in Saskatchewan," *Canadian Tax Journal* Vol.48, No.2 (2000), 374–88. Rushton points to a 1988 income tax study prepared by the Saskatchewan Department of Finance as a precursor to the arguments of the Review Committee. Tax competition with other provinces was not a significant consideration in the earlier study, although it did claim that lower marginal tax rates "provide general support for investment and job creation," while "higher tax rates encourage the transfer of income-earning activity to lower rate jurisdictions." [Province of Saskatchewan, *A Dialogue on Saskatchewan Income Tax Reform* (Regina: Department of Finance, 1988), 6]. In his comparative examination of provincial tax reform initiatives, Geoffrey Hale suggests that "internal political conditions appear to play a larger role in defining the distribution and rate levels of provincial taxes than external tax competition" Hale, "Decentralization…." 255.
30. Final Report… 20.
31. The primary source upon which the Review Committee relies in this respect is Robert D. Brown, "Tax Reform and Tax Reduction: Let's Do the Job Right," *Canadian Tax Journal* Vol.47, No.2 (1999), 182-205. Brown also indicates that, in his view, tax reform and tax reduction are all but identical. Interestingly, he notes as well that the "passion" for tax reform in Canada is significantly less intense than in the United States.

32. Ibid., 22.
33. For a helpful discussion of the ideas of the American political philosopher, John Rawls, whose *Theory of Justice* is considered the most significant contemporary treatment of the question of distributive justice, see Steven M. DeLue, *Political Thinking, Political Theory, and Civil Society* Second Edition (New York: Longman, 2002), ch.13. For a challenging, critical analysis of the issue, see Charles Taylor, "The Nature and Scope of Distributive Justice," in Taylor, *Philosophy and the Human Sciences: Philosophical Papers 2* (Cambridge: Cambridge University Press, 1985), 289–317.
34. Final Report... 26.
35. For a detailed analysis of this claim and the logic underlying it, see Andrea Moe, "Elusive Neutrality: The Recent Debate Surrounding the Child Care Expense Deduction and Income Splitting in Canada," paper presented to the Annual Meeting, Canadian Political Science Association, Laval University, Quebec City, Quebec, May 2001.
36. Final Report... 28.
37. Ibid., 43.
38. It is useful here to distinguish the proposal to treat one- and two-income families equitably from the attempt to gain economic and financial recognition for the unmeasured and unpaid contributions to wellbeing made by a stay-at-home spouse (primarily female). The latter involves more substantial, structural changes beyond alterations to the tax system. At the least, they would require supportive public programs involving, for example, childcare. Funding for such programs is precisely what is threatened by significant tax reductions.
39. Final Report... 23. The Committee's list of "progressive" taxes is interesting in itself. It includes basic personal income tax, flat taxes and surtaxes (Saskatchewan had, until 2001, a deficit-reduction surtax imposed on high income earners). Non-progressive taxes include consumption taxes and health care premiums.
40. In 1971, for example, the federal *Income Tax Act* provided for nineteen tax brackets with a top marginal rate of 82.4 percent applied to taxable income of $400,000 and above (significantly over one million dollars today). According to a November 2000 financial statement issued by the federal government, the rates for 2001 are 17 percent on taxable income up to $30,754; 22 percent on income between $30,754 and $61,509; 26 percent on income between $61,509 and $100,00; and 29 percent on income over $100,000. By 2004 the rates will be 16 percent on income between $8,000 and $35,000; 22 percent on income between $35,000 and $70,000; 26 percent on income between $70,000 and $113,804; and 29 percent on income exceeding $113,804. These latter proposals represent some "stretching" of the existing brackets. But overall, marginal rates are significantly lower and the highest rate applies at a real income level much reduced from what it was in 1971 and earlier. The figures for 1971 come from Gordon Bale "The Carter Report: Good Ideas Remain Good Ideas," in W. Neil Brooks, ed., *The Quest for Tax Reform: The Royal Commission on Taxation Twenty Years Later* (Toronto: Carswell, 1988), 68. The rate proposals are cited in Lisa Philipps, "Women, Taxes and Social Programs," paper presented at "Breakfast on the Hill" Seminar, Humanities and Social Sciences Federation of Canada, Ottawa, ON, April 26, 2001, 3.
41. According to the Committee, both orders of government in Canada, federal and

provincial, relied too heavily on the personal income tax. The Committee cited statistics from the Organization for Economic Cooperation and Development, which indicated that in 1996 personal income tax in Canada stood at 13.9 percent of GDP. This was the highest such figure among the seven major economic powers (the G-7) (Final Report... 31). Of course, by themselves these figures tell us little about the overall tax situation in Canada and elsewhere, to say nothing of the whole issue of the relative roles of private and public sectors.

42. The Committee proposed a three-year transition period for the new system. By 2003–4, Saskatchewan personal income tax rates, applied directly to taxable income, would be 11 percent on income up to $35,000; 13 percent on income between $35,000 and $50,000; and 15 percent on income over $100,000. The 11 percent rate would also apply to capital gains in excess of the current federally established lifetime capital gains exemption. For the 2002 tax year (when this book is being written), the provincial government has established rates of 11.25 percent on the first $30,000; 13.25 percent on the next $30,000; and 15.5 percent on income over $60,000. These are identical to the Committee's proposals.

43. Final Report... 44. One alleged consequence of this move would be to eliminate the anomaly that certain low-income individuals paid exceptionally high real marginal tax rates. This resulted from the combination at certain income levels of higher taxable earnings and reduced income support. For its account of this problem, the Committee relied on the work of University of Regina economist, Michael Rushton. See his "Tax Policy and Income Support: An Analysis of Effective Marginal Tax Rates and Saskatchewan Families," paper presented to Saskatchewan Personal Income Tax Review Committee, June 17, 1999.

44. For a typically acute treatment of this issue, see C.B. Macpherson, *The Political Theory of Possessive Individualism: Hobbes to Locke* (Oxford: Oxford University Press, 1962), 255–7.

45. Hale, *The Politics of Taxation in Canada*, 337.

46. The provincial government has claimed that by 2003, the net cost to the provincial treasury of cuts to personal income taxes will be $260 million. It has suggested that this cost could be financed out of economic growth. Presumably this growth would ensue at least in part from the cuts themselves. "Tax cuts kick in next year," *The Leader-Post* (Regina), December 30, 2000, 1.

47. See Hale, "Decentralization...," which refers to the "growing progressivity of federal and provincial tax systems—in which a large majority of voters receive more in services than they pay in taxes" (255).

48. Friedrich. A. von Hayek, *The Constitution of Liberty* (Chicago: The University of Chicago Press, 1960), 322. Von Mises made a comparable claim: "It is very different for 90 percent of the population to vote taxes on themselves and an exemption of 10 percent than for 90 percent to vote punitive taxes on the other 10 percent.... If a reasonable system of taxation is to be achieved, people must recognize as a principle that the majority which determines what the total amount of taxation should be must also bear it at the maximum rate." (Ludwig von Mises, *Human Action: A Treatise on Economics* (New Haven: Yale University Press, 1949), 803.

Even during the Keynesian era in Canada, these arguments had defenders among influential people. Kenneth Eaton, an important Canadian government tax official in the post-war period, believed that progressive taxation was a product of political expediency whereby governments responded to the electoral demands of low- and middle-income voters by taxing those with high incomes to meet these demands. Indeed, he went further and argued that progressive taxation was ultimately arbitrary because "it is inconsistent with the concept of private property." Kenneth Eaton, *Essays in Taxation* (Toronto: Canadian Tax Foundation, 1966), 27. All passages quoted here are cited in Neil Brooks, "Flattening the Claims of the Flat Taxers," *The Dalhousie Law Journal* 21(2) (Fall 1998), 293, 301.

49. Final Report... 37. Emphasis added.
50. Schumpeter, *Capitalism, Socialism, and Democracy* Third Edition (1950) (New York: Harper Colophon Books, 1975), 83. For an interesting comparison of Keynesian ideas with those of Schumpeter in the context of debates from the nineteen thirties onward about the nature of and prospects for the economy of the United States, see Theodore Rosenof, *Economics in the Long Run: New Deal Theorists and their Legacies, 1933–1993* (Chapel Hill and London: The University of North Carolina Press, 1997), ch.8.
51. W. Leibfritz et al., "Taxation and Economic Performance," *OECD Working Papers*, No.176 (1999); cited in Final Report...38.
52. Final Report... 38. The emphasis is in the original.
53. Bob Jessop, "Towards a Schumpeterian Workfare State? Preliminary Remarks on Post-Fordist Political Economy," *Studies in Political Economy* 40 (Spring 1993), 18–19.
54. See, for example, Final Report... 13, 15.
55. See, for example, Ibid., 16, 18.

Chapter Four

Taxation, the Role of the State and the Dynamics of Political Culture

The reports of the Royal Commission on Taxation and the Saskatchewan Income Tax Review Committee offer contrasting accounts of the nature and function of taxation and the role of the state. Both studies reflected the dominant political values and policy commitments of the periods in which they were undertaken. Both responded to political, fiscal and economic questions that governments of their era felt compelled to address. Some of these were particular to the times. So, for instance, both the McLeod and Vicq committees were created in the context of specific tax reform initiatives emanating from elsewhere. For McLeod, the impetus came from the Carter Commission. For Vicq, it came from highly publicized studies and policies pursued by other governments, notably in Alberta and Ontario.

But it is striking that both reports also confront general issues that in many respects were surprisingly similar in each period: the economic impact of taxation, federal-provincial fiscal relations and, above all, the place of the Saskatchewan economy relative to the rest of the country and the prospects for growth as well as the policies required to promote it. This is because the core question at the heart of a liberal democratic capitalist society is the relation of the state to the market, the polity to the economy. This relationship is always an issue, because there are two distinctive and often competing core principles at work in shaping how the state, or polity, and the market, or economy, operate: for the (democratic) state, one *person*, one vote; for the (capitalist) market, one *dollar*, one vote. Insofar as a society is democratic and capitalist—as Canada was in the 1960s and is today—this relationship remains critical. So both tax studies unavoidably addressed it. In spite of other significant differences between them, in this, at least, they shared common ground.

Of course, how this relationship is understood and managed can and does vary over time. This is what the shift from Keynesianism to neo-liberalism, two different approaches to the respective roles of state and market, represents. Because these approaches both reflected and helped shape this relationship, each became at different points in time conventional wisdom and formed a central component of how people viewed the world, particularly those individuals who recommend or make policy. It may hardly seem surprising that all three members of the Review Committee, including the Chair, were chartered accountants, who might be expected to hold pro-free market views on taxation, especially in a period when such views had become influential. But, as earlier noted, Thomas McLeod, who chaired the Royal Commission, was Dean of the College of Commerce at the University of Saskatchewan, while the other two Commissioners were a chartered accountant and a lawyer.¹ Commerce, law and accountancy are obviously linked closely to the workings of a market economy, in which financial considerations play a crucial role. If it is realistic to assume that individuals from those professions represent the most influential ideological views in a capitalist society, this provides even stronger evidence of how these views have shifted.

Quite apart from the specific claims and recommendations of the two studies, there are also passages in the reports that suggest both bodies had some sense of the larger political context, and context of ideas, within which they worked. Because of both its assumptions and the scope of its inquiry (the two are related), the McLeod Commission was more self-conscious and fulsome in this respect. But even the more narrowly focused Vicq Report on occasion alluded to concerns greater than marginal tax rates.

As was discussed in Chapter Two, the Royal Commission sought to account for and justify the increasingly prominent role of the state in the economy. It traced this to the historical development of industrial society and the interdependence between the state and the market this created. There was a certain element of inevitability in this account, a sense that social development and its related interdependence were bound to lead to a greater and more widely accepted role for the state, because such a role was a rational response to an increasingly complex economic and social order. Objective interdependence would produce an increasingly crucial role for the state, sanctioned by democratic electorates committed to extensive government expenditures. The expanded state would be tolerated and even supported by a business community no longer composed of fiercely individualistic entrepreneurs hostile to government but rather of corporate managers who understood the necessity for collective organization. The values and institutions of the Keynesian welfare state epitomized this process and as a consequence were here to stay.

We now know that subsequent opposition to the Keynesian welfare state and the emergence of neo-liberal ideology and policy shattered this logic. It *was* possible to turn back the clock and revive earlier, apparently moribund values of "free enterprise" and *laissez-faire*, or limited government.²

Yet the Royal Commission was not entirely wrong. There *is* greater interdependence, even in the era of neo-liberalism and its individualist values. Fashionable notions about globalization and the emergence of an international "risk society" implicitly acknowledge this. The idea of a "risk society" involves "an emerging global technological world which generates a diversity of possible dangers, hazards, and futures" that cross political boundaries and social boundaries as well—for example, if ecological disaster strikes, rich and poor alike will be affected.³ What occurs anywhere could affect life everywhere.

So, what happened? How did a reinvigorated individualism come to the fore in the face of interdependence? The answer, I suggest, illuminates not only the different assumptions underlying each tax study but also something about the qualities of everyday thought and action as manifested in the terms under which people are encouraged to think about themselves and their society.

With its individualist commitments, on the one hand, and its need to make sense of an interdependent world where no one is an island on oneself, on the other, neo-liberalism simultaneously promotes and expresses a state of affairs that is a source of tension in the lives of individuals. The tension results from the rupturing of what might be called the objective and the subjective elements of social life, that is, social institutions and practices, on the one hand, and how people are encouraged to view these and themselves and therefore how they should act, on the other. This is a matter of both philosophy and social experience. Insofar as institutions and practices are made to conform to neo-liberal values and individuals are encouraged or required to act as rational choosers and competitors, the worlds of both thought and practice become divided, internally contradictory.

The contradiction arises from the reality that, in the end, the objective will triumph: interdependence cannot literally be willed away. The terms with which we understand the world and ourselves are part of a language that is unavoidably shared. We become persons together with other persons; we need others to recognize us, and we need to recognize others in the course of recognizing ourselves. The "I" always supposes a "we." Even in an era in which individualism is triumphant, society, as the condition and context of individual identity, asserts its presence. This can be seen from the fact that, even under the impact of neo-liberalism, the contemporary state, either in Canada or elsewhere, is hardly disappearing. "Freeing" the market is an act of deliberate policy not a passive response to an irresistible fact of nature. It is states, and the governments which speak for them, that have tied their own hands by enacting international trade deals, such as the North American Free Trade Agreement (NAFTA), and by strengthening or creating international organizations charged with the task of imposing market discipline, including the International Monetary Fund (IMF) and the World Trade Organization (WTO). Indeed, some argue that trade agreements in the context of which international organizations operate are "full-fledged frameworks of economic integration" which "function as economic constitutions, setting the basic rules governing private property rights that all governments must respect and the types of economic policies that all governments must eschew."⁴ This self-imposed limitation applies as well to domestic policies of privatization and deregulation designed to permit domestic markets to function in an unimpeded way.

In his *Leviathan*, Thomas Hobbes claimed that *"the NATURALL CONDITION of Mankind,"* was pre-social and radically individualist, characterized at its extreme by a war of all against all, a competitive struggle for survival.[5] Hobbes intended this as an argument in response to the question why people ought to obey political authority, since they 'naturally' would rather do want they wanted without limits, that is, pursue their self-interested desires without restraint. He hoped to provide a compelling reason why, for individuals, it was actually in their self-interest, and thus rational, to restrict self-interest and live together with mutual obligations in a political community.

In a manner of speaking, the neo-liberal state promotes a kind of Hobbesian "state of nature," an enforced disavowal of connectedness and community.[6] This means denying certain personal motives which incline people to embrace a more comprehensive understanding of community beyond the ties of the market. Such motives arguably had more of a place in the Keynesian era.

The McLeod Commission could assume and defend the idea, and reality, that the individual did not stand so far apart from the collective, that personal and communal wellbeing implied each other. *As a result, taxation could not simply be viewed as a burden, a limitation on personal freedom, particularly economic freedom.* Quite apart from the political and ideological consensus it represented at the time, the Royal Commission could be comprehensive in its treatment of taxation policy within its social and political backdrop because the social, the communal, was a real force in its own right. It was not merely a vehicle for otherwise isolated or atomistic individuals to realize allegedly self-contained purposes.

In this light, other than the simple desire to justify tax cuts, there may have been a reason for the narrow structure of the later Review Committee report. We have seen that the Committee held a view of the social order that was individualist but also instrumentalist, that is, people calculated wellbeing in light of the means, or instruments (including other people), available for the achievement of their ends. But the objective nature of our social ties cannot be willed away so easily. The narrowness of the Committee's analysis may have reflected how difficult it was to find a place therein for communal sensibilities.

Stated differently, while neo-liberalism has to a considerable extent become dominant or hegemonic, this hegemony is less secure than that of Keynesianism during the post-war era.[7] Neo-liberal ideas have not been uncontested. Committed free marketers are apt to argue that dissent comes from "special interests," because such groups have a vested interest in big government. But in fact neo-liberalism is incapable of accounting for, and making sense of, important elements of individual experience, commitments and expectations: those associated with ties that are other than instrumental and are beyond the claims of the market.

In an account of the nature of common or public goods, that is, goods provided by the state, the Canadian political philosopher, Charles Taylor, distinguishes between "convergent" and both "mediate" and "immediate" common goods. This matters because while most people, even committed free marketers, might agree that the organized political community exists to pursue certain common, collective or public goods, there are important differences in the "publicness" of goods. Convergent public goods are collectively provided goods whose desirability does not reside in their being so offered. In principle, individuals would provide these for themselves if they could, and the nature of such goods would not be altered in any way. Examples here include national defence and police and fire protection. All other goods are assumed to be private; in this view, they can (and probably should) be offered through the market. Standing behind this position is the further assumption that political societies "are established by collections of individuals to obtain benefits through common action that they could not secure individually. The action is collective, but the point of it remains individual. The common good is constituted out of individual goods without remainder."[8] In short, society is an instrument for individuals who occasionally find it necessary to act together in pursuit of goals that are otherwise private and of value to each alone, one by one.

By contrast, mediate and immediate public goods are goods whose public character, the fact they are provided collectively, is either part or all of what makes them goods. Mediate common or public goods have a private character in that they could be and often are enjoyed alone by individuals separately but are enriched, and even transformed, by being shared. Taylor uses as examples the telling of a joke or listening to music. It also applies to the world of diplomacy among states, where something unsaid or only discretely acknowledged takes on a different character when it becomes public, for then people have to react to it. Debates about government (and corporate) secrecy clearly turn on this. It's probably no coincidence that the move to the private sector, economically and politically, under the impact of neo-liberalism seems to be matched by a renewed emphasis by governments on secrecy and a waning of the commitment to publicity, however limited, that followed in the wake of the enactment in the 1970s and 1980s of freedom of information legislation.

Immediate common goods are defined just by the fact they are provided in common. It's not that they would lose something if enjoyed by one person alone; they wouldn't exist at all unless they were enjoyed together. Friendship is an obvious example; so perhaps are the bonds of family. Politically, "solidarity" has this character. Under the bonds of solidarity, there is a merging of fates, so that the ability of one to realize his or her purpose is inextricably tied to the ability of all to do so. And only when they achieve their common aims together do people fulfill themselves individually.

Traditionally, in contrast to the conception of the political community as founded on a social contract between otherwise isolated individuals, the idea of solidarity has been associated with a republican model of politics. In a republican political community, active citizens govern themselves under laws and institutions which do not merely regulate their actions but define or express widely and deeply held common purposes not reducible to the aggregation of individual aims. In Taylor's words: "This can only be a willing identification with the polis on the part of the citizens, a sense that the political institutions in which they live are an expression of themselves. The 'laws' have to be seen as reflecting and entrenching their dignity as citizens, and hence to be in a sense extensions of themselves."[9] In short, the political community itself is an immediate common good.

So whether common or public goods are seen as mediate or immediate, their value is constituted by the fact that they *are* common. They exist as shared goods. They are goods not just for you or for me, but for *us*. Common goods are not in this view discrete, "consumable" objects but rather patterns of interaction which bring people together in certain structured ways. They suggest a common life or a life of common engagements.

In contrast to the social contract idea of the political community, which accords with much of what we take for granted as common sense about politics, the republican model might appear utopian or unrealistic. No doubt, in its so-called classical form associated with ancient Greece, republican Rome and Renaissance Italy (notably Machiavelli's beloved Florence), it is. Modern societies are much more extensively and widely individualistic (and, it should be added, at least in principle, more egalitarian) than were those. But the distinction between the two parallels, informs and is informed by the distinction, discussed in Chapter One, between democracy as a system for choosing governments and democracy as a kind of society; or between representative democracy and its participatory alternative. This is because individuals, one by one, undertake the act of voting that forms the core of representative democracy, and election results come from adding up the votes to see who has "won." Such an act is neither collective nor, typically, very participatory. Thus it accords more with the social contract account than the republican one.

That there is periodic disenchantment with representative democracy and the desire for more active, participatory forms suggests that, even in a liberal democratic, capitalist political culture, with its roots primarily in the social contract model, there are republican aspirations which surface from time to time. In Canada, quite apart from attitudes toward democracy and disaffection with existing governments and the political process as a whole, there is some sense of this in the ongoing debate about Medicare. Commitment to Medicare seems to be about more than just a matter of how health care is provided. It appears that it is widely seen as an element of citizenship. In other words, it is not merely useful but valuable, and valuable for people together and not just for each separately. This is why attempts, exceptionally vigorous at the moment, to transform Medicare into more of a private, market-based system, seem doomed to fail. Proponents of greater "privatization" appeal to self-interest. But most people have more than a self-interested commitment to it. Medicare exudes at least a whiff of republicanism.

There are two points I want to note about the question of common or public goods, and thus of goods not delivered, or not deemed capable of being delivered, through the market. First of all, while the conceptual distinction between public and private goods or between convergent and mediate or immediate public goods is clear enough, in practice, the boundaries demarking them are socially and historically variable. It is not the specific characteristics of goods that define them as public or private. It is their social form—the institutions, practices and values under which they are produced—that determines their location in either the public or private sector. This is the outcome of the constellation of political and social forces and ideas at work at any point in time. Contemporary political and policy debates shaped by the emergence of neo-liberalism make this particularly clear. Neo-liberals have sought to redraw the boundaries between public and private goods in a radical way, to the point of challenging the public character of goods that even a previous generation of conservative defenders of the market had by and large taken for granted or at least generally accepted. Examples include services such as police and fire protection and public power utilities, for decades defined as essential public goods. The current debate about Medicare also displays some of this. But it is especially visible in the attempt to define public goods such as education as potentially marketable commodities and hence, in principle, private. We can see this process at work as well in the character of current political language—terms such as "consumer," "stakeholder" and even "taxpayer" reflect a diminished idea of the "public."

This relates in turn to a second point, which may help us understand something of the nature of the Keynesian welfare state and the shift to neo-liberalism. There is no doubt that during the Keynesian era, the public sector expanded dramatically: the range and extent of public goods was significantly broadened. Yet, arguably, the lion's share of such goods was convergent and not immediate. To be sure, the Keynesian welfare state represented what I suggested at the beginning of this chapter was a core question for modern liberal democracy: the working out of the relation, or compromise, between capitalism and democracy. With the capitalist economy playing the dominant role, obviously many of the public goods pursued by the welfare state would be of a convergent character, since historically such goods have proven compatible with the logic of capitalism and the market.

On the other hand, if I am correct about the variable nature of the boundary not only between public and private goods but also, just as importantly, between convergent and immediate public goods, then the specifically public character of goods widely recognized *as* public is not necessarily fixed. In other words, if it is possible to conceive public goods *per se* as private, as neo-liberalism is wont to do, then it is also possible to consider *convergent* public goods as *immediate* public goods.

In my view, the Keynesian welfare state, as it developed particularly in Canada and the United States, tended to create or expand public goods that were primarily convergent, but which in principle could have been established as immediate. This may offer insight into both the character of the welfare state and its historical fate over the course of the last four decades. For what is at stake is the question of whether people see the public realm as an instrument for their private purposes or as a shared set of meanings and practices binding them together with others. To take an example: programs of social assistance, the "welfare" so closely identified with the welfare state, were typically designed and administered as income support measures for individuals considered one by one as income earners, who required enhanced means to fulfill their individual economic needs. It was delivered by a bureaucratic apparatus in the hands of "experts," functioning according to professional norms of service delivery. The bureaucratic state was a kind of stand-in for the market and just as impersonal and inescapable. Indeed, in the 1960s and 1970s, these qualities of the state led to criticisms of it as rigid and unresponsive from all points on the ideological spectrum. (That private sector, or market-driven, institutions have usually escaped such criticisms reflects the reality that these are widely presented as, and understood as, both facts of nature and embodiments of freedom.)

In short, welfare had the earmarks of a convergent public good. There were those who paid for the programs through taxes and those who received benefits. But there was little connection between these two groups, save through the medium of the state that collected the taxes and delivered the services. Defence of these programs tended to be instrumental: income assistance allowed recipients to purchase goods and services, and this supported aggregate demand in the economy and hence the jobs upon which most taxpayers depended for their incomes. While this was true, it represented a limited justification. There was little if any attempt to defend them on grounds of solidarity: that they made possible the inclusion in society of people otherwise excluded and that this strengthened the social bond, created a "public" that was more than just individuals added together. In other words, there was little effort to treat welfare as an immediate, as opposed to convergent, public good.

This has had consequences for the subsequent transformation of the welfare state under neo-liberal auspices. Once economic growth, employment and incomes declined, and neo-liberal ideas took hold, the model of the stakeholder, or taxpayer, the "self-reliant" individual, triumphed over that of the citizen prepared to sustain economic support for the less fortunate, if not to share self-conscious bonds of solidarity with them. Many people began to view income assistance as unjust. They saw it as taking money from hardworking, productive individuals and squandering it on the unworthy. They began to withdraw their support from the welfare state. This was evident in the election of governments committed to its "reform" along more market-friendly lines.[10] With respect to recipients, the levels of support, although in real terms more significant thirty years ago than now, were never fully adequate, and the way the programs were delivered did not work to broaden participation in the society and the state, to enhance inclusion or citizenship.

The point here is that there is nothing in the nature of the case that made income support a convergent public good. It was a political decision, not necessarily consciously intended by anyone in particular but nonetheless enshrined in policy choices, to so treat it. Welfare is a good example of a process that tended to occur across the board. To put it starkly: in its heyday, the welfare state in principle could have been established on republican and participatory lines. It was instead founded on contractarian, bureaucratic and largely non-participatory foundations (although, as the case of Medicare makes clear, it was not without some elements of republicanism).

Of course, whether or not the welfare state actually could have, in the circumstances, been republican is another matter. The answer to this question turns on the relative weight of contending political, social and ideological forces in play at the time, primarily the comparative strength of those groups committed to the *status quo* (predominantly business) and those committed to greater equality (the labour movement in particular, but also and increasingly women, and ethnic and racial minorities), and the forms of political language available to people for understanding themselves and their society. Given the configuration of forces in liberal democratic capitalist societies, especially Canada and the U.S., perhaps no other choice *was* possible: the capitalist principle of "one dollar, one vote" was stronger than the democratic claim of "one person, one vote." As noted above, convergent public goods fit better with the logic of a capitalist market society. Nonetheless, recognizing what was at stake may still be helpful in clarifying questions about the individual and the community, questions central to "embedded political theory."

To be sure, whatever its particular characteristics and limitations, the Keynesian welfare state still helped construct a public and something of a sense of bonding, even if under the limiting constraints of convergent public goods. After all, convergent public goods are still "public." This may explain why "social cohesion," the preserving of social bonds that allow for people to cooperate harmoniously, has lately emerged as a serious concern in both official and academic circles. There is the fear that the ties binding people together in societies, which have become increasingly fragmented and individualistic, are fraying, that there is diminution of "social capital": "connections among individuals—social networks and norms of reciprocity and trustworthiness that arise from them."[11] Social cohesion could be seen as having been embedded in the very practices, institutions and commitments of the Keynesian welfare state, however limited the welfare state might have been by virtue of its character as a an array of convergent public goods. It was never singled out and defined as a "problem." This can only occur when individualism begins to get out of hand and produce socially— and individually—unacceptable consequences, which themselves result from both the active encouragement of, and absence of restraint on, competitive individualism, itself.

This is one of the lessons to be learned from the recent wave of corporate scandals, particularly in the U.S., where executives of companies such as the energy trading corporation, Enron, consciously cashed in on company stocks even as the companies themselves were failing, with callous disregard for their employees and the communities where they lived and worked.[12] It is probably no coincidence that such corporations have tended to be "hollowed out": employees are treated as, and encouraged to think of themselves as, independent contractors and not as participants sharing in a common endeavour from which they could draw ongoing support. The notion of a corporate "body," which made corporations in the Keynesian era rather like small communities (this process was significantly more advanced in countries such as Germany, Sweden and Japan in the post-war period), has to a considerable extent been a casualty of the rise of neo-liberalism and neo-liberal globalization.[13]

All this provided the context within which the Saskatchewan Personal Income Tax Review Committee did its work, a context the Committee did not of course spell out. Because it was not self-consciously ideological, its neo-liberalism more in the form of taken-for-granted assumptions, the Committee did not defend neo-liberal ideas explicitly. As indicated above, it tended to focus overwhelmingly on marginal tax rates and individual responses to these, leaving out issues of politics and community that did not fit with current thinking about the place of markets and governments. Of course, this was in part a reflection of the Committee's narrow terms of reference.

Yet because of the nature of tax questions and the fact that, during the course of its public hearings, neo-liberal prescriptions for taxation and economic policy were contested, the Committee was compelled to address the tension between neo-liberalism and community. The Final Report contains the following interesting passage:

> The Committee was somewhat concerned that, for the most part, the submissions made to the Committee were polarized at one end

of a spectrum (those wanting significant tax cuts) or the other (those wanting increases in taxes to fund additional social programs or infrastructure). We heard very few voices for a *balanced* approach to change. This has made our job difficult.[14]

The claim that "balance" was a problem for the Committee is instructive. The Committee saw a split between tax "cutters" and program "spenders." This suggests that taxing and spending are distinct activities informed by different requirements and purposes, yet the separation of taxing and spending in this way disconnects two dimensions of fiscal policy, how revenue is raised and what it is used for, that are in reality closely linked and even inseparable. This involves more than simply the question of the efficient allocation of resources, on the one side, and the prudent and accountable expenditure of public funds, on the other. In other words, taxation isn't simply about raising cash, or spending, just about providing services to individual citizen-consumers. Taxing and spending are essential elements of a modern body politic. In a society in which organized economic activity expresses fundamental human purposes, as most assuredly our capitalist market social order does, taxing and spending articulate different relations persons share with each other through the medium of the state. These help define where people stand in relation to the market and the state. The question of who pays taxes and who benefits from expenditures is clearly part of this. But so, too, are issues involving more personal kinds of identity. This is a complex matter, but to take just two examples: taxing and spending can affect occupational identities (some people work for governments and are paid with the proceeds of taxation), and they can affect cultural identities (for example through multicultural programs people are given the opportunity to preserve or develop specific cultural values and practices). This is why political and economic factors have to be considered together, as political economy. And political economy deals not only with facts and institutions, but also has a significant normative, or moral, dimension. It deals with the formation of personal identities and what is important for those who bear these identities.[15]

In the end, taxation can never be solely about efficiency; whatever its other limitations, in the heyday of the Keynesian welfare state, this was more widely accepted and incorporated into tax policy. Taxation also necessarily addresses issues such as redistribution and stabilization, even if they are rarely these days considered the appropriate targets of tax measures. Taxation substantively fills out the meaning of property rights in society—it helps define who owns what and what these owners may do with their holdings, at least with respect to what they can do for "themselves" and what they are required to do for the society as a whole. It shapes access to resources. As a result, it redistributes life chances even if redistribution *per se*, and in particular egalitarian redistribution, is not a policy goal. And since stabilization policy involves regulating the potentially chaotic cycles to which a capitalist economy is prone, abandonment of this policy entails government decisions and actions to "insititutionalize" the *in*stability of uncontrolled market forces. This, too, creates a Hobbesian state of nature, a condition of pervasive insecurity.

The perspective of the Committee supports a certain view of the relation of empirical to normative concerns in tax policy, that is, the relation of facts about society to values concerned with what society should be like. The "reality" of the market, the "necessity" of acknowledging individual self-seeking behaviour as the only genuine and inescapable foundation of economic activity, is seen as the empirical "truth" by which state taxation initiatives must abide. No "real" possibilities exist outside this framework. Any other conception of the nature of human productive activity is an ideologically motivated flight of fancy.

If this claim is accepted, there are two possible normative responses. One position, that of the most rabid free marketers, is that the very "reality" of the market is its own normative justification, because it is the basis and outcome of free, individual choices. Governments have no right to interfere.[16] To use the language of classical, eighteenth- and nineteenth-century political economy, the market system is one of "natural liberty." The other position accepts the possibility of subjecting market outcomes, how the market economy distributes resources, to external normative judgments, that is, judgments rooted in values that are more than economic or market-based. But, to be "realistic,"such judgments must accept the primacy of those outcomes. Hence, normative issues represent "deviations" from an otherwise ideal standard of market justice. These deviations should be minimized as fully as possible. This position seemed to be that of the Review Committee.

But an alternative view, to which Keynesianism was much closer, would not countenance this way of understanding the empirical and the normative. This other view is rooted in a conception of institutions as historical and dynamic, and not ahistorical or static. The state in capitalist society has come to play a central economic role, as the Royal Commission recognized. Once the process of historical development had made it evident that "the market" was not, nor could be, self-regulating, the image of a timeless, rational, self-contained, utility maximizing individual could no longer represent the unchallenged 'truth' of human behaviour.[17] Insofar as this conception of human purpose *has* come to express individual aspirations and actions and thus constitutes "reality," it has to be pressed against, and win out against, other possibilities. People don't just "naturally" accept market values uncritically, as if these were facts of nature and beyond challenge. Indeed they can (and frequently do) resist when they believe that too much of individual and social life is treated as if everything exists solely to be bought and sold. One of the great books of the twentieth century, Karl

Polanyi's *The Great Transformation*, is precisely about this: how in response to the rise to prominence of the market economy in nineteenth-century European societies, people challenged its dominance in the name of non-market values.[18] If, in the face of this response, the notion of human beings as essentially rational utility maximizers is incorporated into the values and practices of society, this means that it has been established politically, as part of the process whereby disagreements about conflicting social options are resolved. Politics is about human choices, the exercise of human will. It involves judgments about what is or is not appropriate. Thus, empirical accounts of how people actually behave are necessarily normative as well. The facts of political life embody values because these facts are created through human choices about things that matter to us.

This means that it is not possible to simply describe human behaviour, as if one were studying a microbe under a microscope or charting the movement of a celestial body through a high-powered telescope. To describe what people do, using the language people use both to explain and understand human actions, theirs and others', is to evaluate it. We are not neutral toward human activity; indeed, the very term "human" is both a descriptive and a normative concept. If the facts of human behaviour are always at the same time normative, then this behaviour is malleable. It can no longer be viewed as an unchanging edifice built on timeless foundations. Its "truths" are dynamic. They have been and can be transformed. This occurs as individuals, using the cultural terms available to them, the dominant ideas about what is appropriate and realistic, confront their circumstances and the demands these impose. These circumstances are social and historical—they emerge over the course of the development of human capacities and relationships. They are the products of the responses by people to the options they confront, by which in turn they generate new ones.[19]

The Report of the Royal Commission on Taxation conveyed a sense of this developmental understanding of social and economic institutions and practices. As noted earlier, the Commission saw taxation as embedded in a set of practices associated with a necessary and growing role for the state. Issues relating to the efficient allocation of resources could not be divorced from the question "efficiency for what?" Otherwise put, the matter of allocation did not turn on how to justify deviations from the "ideal", that is, a fully market-driven process of allocation. Both market *and* state were viewed as essential allocative mechanisms *in their own right*. Of course, the mix of state and market mechanisms varied both from country to country and from time to time, and this profoundly shaped the political economy of each polity.[20] Nonetheless, it was taken for granted there was an essential place for both.

Because it moved within this framework of thinking, the Royal Commission report suggested a rich and challenging approach to taxation. The raising and spending of revenue was about more than government accounts.

It conveyed a sense of how economic relations in a capitalist market society could be subject to regulation. Market forces are humanly created and humanly driven. Their "force" stems from human desire and will; unregulated market behaviour is about unconstrained human desire taking the form, as Hobbes clearly understood, of the desire for power over others. Taxation (as well as expenditure) is political and not just in the sense that in levying taxes governments respond to pressures from political interests. More fundamentally, it is a mechanism by which otherwise self-seeking individuals, in a culture that is in important ways individualistic, can come to recognize the reality of connectedness. In a complex and diverse liberal democratic capitalist society, it may indeed be one of the few ways in which this recognition can come about. In its comments about public provisioning, the Royal Commission seemed to convey this, even if (as was likely) this was not its specific intent.

By contrast, the Final Report of the Personal Income Tax Review Committee seems flat, even impoverished. This is not because it was prepared by (or for) accountants. Rather, it has to do with the assumptions it accepted. In contrast, the McLeod Commission seemed to take for granted a kind of social and historical "density"; it gave the impression that it was difficult to discuss important political and economic questions without a sense of historical and social context. Again, this is more a question of the language of analysis than of conscious purpose. It is the *how* of the McLeod Commission's account, not just the *what*. With its implicit commitment to the assumptions of rational choice, the Vicq Committee had little conceptual space to raise questions of taxation in the same manner as did the McLeod Commission. There is certainly coherence to the rational-choice view of individuals. But just as there is a price paid in the realm of lived experience for disavowing or denying connectedness, so, too, there is a price paid in the domain of intellectual or policy analysis. I think the Vicq report paid this price.

I indicated above that taxation is a way individuals can come to recognize connectedness. The operative word here is "can." There is no guarantee they will do so. Indeed, given the dominant view of this matter these days, they, or at least many of them, do not (cannot? will not?), even if most people more or less accept the necessity of paying their taxes. So, are Vicq and rational choice correct? It is possible to grant there is truth to the individualist view, while at the same time suggesting this could never be the whole truth, that there is always something more going on than such a perspective can convey; indeed much of this chapter has been devoted to developing this point. But to fully defend this idea requires a further exploration of political language in the context of the tax studies, an excursion into the realm of what I call "embedded political theory." For, while the two reports illuminated the differences between Keynesianism and neo-liberalism, as important as these differences are, there is more at stake.

Notes

1. As indicated above, McLeod was an important official in CCF and later NDP governments, while Jack Vicq had served as a researcher for the Royal Commission.
2. See Harold Chorney and Phillip Hansen, "Neo-conservatism, social democracy and 'province building': The experience of Manitoba," *Canadian Review of Sociology and Anthropology* Vol.22, No.1 (February 1985), 1–29.
3. Anthony Elliott, "Introduction," in Anthony Elliott, ed., *The Blackwell Reader in Contemporary Social Theory* (Oxford: Blackwell Publishers, 1999), 15. For more extensive treatment of this idea, see, for example, Ulrich Beck, *World Risk Society* (Cambridge: Polity Press, 1999); see also Anthony Giddens, *Beyond Left and Right: The Future of Radical Politics* (Stanford, CA: Stanford University Press, 1994). For a comprehensive treatment the question of risk and of the many dimensions of globalization generalization, see David Held et al., *Global Transformations: Politics, Economics and Culture* (Cambridge: Polity Press, 1999), esp. ch.8; and David Held and Anthony McGrew (eds.), *The Global Transformation Reader: An Introduction to the Globalization Debate* (Cambridge: Polity Press, 2000).
4. Ian Robinson, "The NAFTA, Democracy and Continental Economic Integration: Trade Policy as if Democracy Mattered," in Susan D. Phillips, ed., *How Ottawa Spends 1993–1994: A More Democratic Canada…?* (Ottawa: Carleton University Press, 1993), 334. For a detailed treatment of this issue and its implications for the Canadian state and political community as a whole, see Stephen Clarkson, *Uncle Sam and Us: Globalization, Neoconservatism, and the Canadian State* (Toronto and Washington, DC: University of Toronto Press and Woodrow Wilson Center Press, 2002), esp. ch.4.
5. Thomas Hobbes, *Leviathan* (1651), ed. by C.B. Macpherson (London: Penguin Books, 1988), esp. part I, ch.XIII.
6. For a striking account of the consequences of organizing society as if it were a state of nature, in this case the primary heartland of free market values, the United States, see Frank M. Coleman, *Hobbes and America: Exploring the Constitutional Foundations* (Toronto and Buffalo: University of Toronto Press, 1977).
7. Another way to put this: while Keynesianism has the more powerful ideas, neo-liberalism has the more powerful supporters.
8. Charles Taylor, "Cross-Purposes: The Liberal-Communitarian Debate," in Nancy Rosenblum, ed., *Liberalism and the Moral Life* (Cambridge, MA: Harvard University Press, 1989), 166.
9. Ibid.,165. For a useful discussion of republican ideas, see David Held, *Models of Democracy* Second Edition (Cambridge: Polity Press, 1996), ch.2.
10. For a comprehensive treatment of this issue of "defection" from support of the welfare state, see the work of the German social theorist, Claus Offe, for example, "Democracy Against the Welfare State?" in *Modernity and the State: East, West* (Cambridge, MA: The MIT Press, 1996), ch.8; and "Interdependence, Difference and Limited State Capacity" in Glen Drover and Patrick Kerans (eds.), *New Approaches to Welfare Theory* (Aldershot, Eng.: Edward Elgar, 1993), 235–41. For Canada, there is interesting statistical evidence that may at least in part reflect this development and its consequences. Social spending,

defined as government transfers to individuals to improve their incomes or provide social services, declined from 12.7 percent of GDP in 1993 (a recession year) to 9.3 per cent in 2000. While some of this decline could doubtless be attributed to falling unemployment (social spending tends to vary with the unemployment rate, and the national unemployment rate fell approximately three percentage points during this period), in 2000 the unemployment rate was still in excess of seven per cent: the decline in social spending seemed to exceed what would normally have been expected given the level of unemployment. Interestingly, the decline in social spending was in the context of recent history unique. Over the course of several decades, the only comparable decline was in the period between 1934 and 1942, when Canada moved from the very high unemployment rates of the Great Depression to what was virtually total full employment in a wartime economy. See Bruce Little, "Social spending now following a new pattern," *The Globe and Mail* (Toronto), November 18, 2002, B2.

11. Robert Putnam, *Bowling Alone: The Collapse and Revival of American Community* (New York: Simon and Schuster, 2000), 19. This book has become an almost instant academic "classic" in the United States and is often cited by politicians and policymakers. For a collection of studies dealing with various dimensions and implications of Putnam's account, see Scott L. McLean, David A. Schultz, and Manfred B. Steger, eds., *Social Capital: Critical Perspectives on Community and "Bowling Alone"* (New York and London: New York University Press, 2002).

12. Robin Blackburn, "The Enron Debacle and the Pension Crisis," *New Left Review* 14 (March-April 2002), 26–51.

13. Blackburn cites an interesting passage from a 1999 Fortune magazine article by a prominent American economist, Paul Krugman, who had recently joined the advisory board of Enron. Krugman noted, with apparent approval, that in the wake of its transformation from a pipeline operator to an energy trading enterprise, "the company's pride and joy is a room filled with hundreds of casually dressed men and women staring at computer screens and barking into telephones, where cubic feet and megawatts are traded and packaged as if they were financial derivatives [i.e. purely financial products as opposed to real goods and services].... The whole scene looks as if it had been constructed to illustrate the end of the corporation as we know it." Ibid., 27.

14. Final Report...13. Emphasis added.

15. For a classic statement of this position, see Jean-Jacques Rousseau, "A Discourse on Political Economy" (1755), in J.-J.Rousseau, *The Social Contract and Discourses* trans. and introduced by G.D.H. Cole; rev. and augmented by J.H. Brumfit and John C. Hall; updated by P.D. Jimack (London: J. M. Dent, 1993), 128–77.

16. A contemporary classic statement of this position is Robert Nozick, *Anarchy, State, and Utopia* (New York: Basic Books, 1974). As Nozick argues: "Individuals have rights, and there are things no person or group may do to them (without violating their rights). So strong and far-reaching are these rights that they raise the question of what, if anything, the state and its officials may do" (ix). People have the unlimited right to dispose of their possessions as they see fit; free exchange in the marketplace is how this is normally done. Thus, redistributive taxation is a violation of their fundamental rights. For a discussion of this

"libertarian" argument and its defence of the virtually unlimited right of acquisition (i.e. private property), see Will Kymlicka, *Contemporary Political Philosophy: An Introduction* Second Edition (Toronto: Oxford University Press, 2002), ch.4.
17. For a brilliant account of the relation of the historical development of capitalism to conceptions of human nature, see C.B. Macpherson, "The Deceptive Task of Political Theory" (1954), in Macpherson, *Democratic Theory: Essays in Retrieval*, 195–203.
18. Karl Polanyi, *The Great Transformation* (1944) (Boston: Beacon Press, 1957).
19. For an interesting discussion of this question, see Anne Mayhew, "Human Agency, Cumulative Causation, and the State," *Journal of Economic Issues* Vol. XXV. No. 2 (June 2001), 239–50.
20. For an account of the different effects of Keynesian ideas in different states, see Peter.A. Hall (ed.), *The Political Power of Economic Ideas: Keynesianism Across Nations* (Princeton, NJ: Princeton University Press, 1989).

Chapter Five

A Tale of Two Studies:
"Embedded Political Theory" and Democracy

The reports of the McLeod Commission and the Vicq Committee reflect the shift from Keynesianism to neo-liberalism over the course of the past three decades and, thus, distinctive and competing conceptions of appropriate policy. Their respective views of taxation clearly demonstrate this. While the McLeod report held that existing and even prospectively higher rates of taxation were at least compatible with economic prosperity, the Vicq report claimed that taxes had to be reduced to ensure prosperity.

The shift was also reflected by the changed political climate as well. It is noteworthy that CCF or NDP governments undertook both studies. By the time the Royal Commission reported in 1965, a Liberal government under Ross Thatcher had replaced the CCF in office. Rhetorically at least, the new government was significantly to the right of its CCF predecessor and vigorously promoted a free market agenda. (This soon brought it into conflict with its federal Liberal counterpart.) Whether because of its focus and recommendations or because it was associated with a political opponent, the McLeod Commission report was essentially shelved.[1]

We cannot, therefore, know for certain what a CCF government would have done in 1965. But we do know that the current NDP-led government has embraced the main recommendations of the Vicq Committee. It has moved to direct taxation of personal income and has adopted the Committee's proposed rate structure. Social democracy in Saskatchewan has undoubtedly shifted in a more conservative direction over the course of the last four decades.[2]

But as interesting as the change in the political climate in Saskatchewan or even the in larger capitalist world might be, an examination of the two tax studies and tax policy generally provides us with more. It gives clues about the character of political institutions, political values and prospects for political change.

This book has focused not only on the specific analyses and recommendations of the two reports but also on the conceptual logic informing them. Each study suggests a view of the political community. Each defines a framework for thinking about empirically possible and normatively appropriate value commitments, social practices and government policies. The language of each orients us to what is both familiar and strange. It allows us to distinguish between what we can accept, because it "fits" with our sense of what matters to us as agents who harbour certain wants, needs and purposes, and what we cannot. The tax studies help define the limits of the political imagination at different points in time. In the sense that we live *through* language and not just *with* it, the ideas in the reports are not "just" ideas, terms we create to deal with "external" reality. Language simultaneously discloses and constitutes the world, including the world of our purposes and actions. It does not simply represent or capture it. The Canadian political philosopher, Charles Taylor, who builds here on the work of the German philosopher, Martin Heidegger, nicely puts it this way: "[L]anguage ... opens access to meanings. Language discloses.... The disclosure is not intrapsychic, but occurs in the space between humans; indeed, it helps to define the space that humans share."[3] There are two especially critical points here: language is inherently collective or political (because it is not just something going on in our heads, not "intrapsychic," but discloses "in the space between humans"); and it exists in use, and is thus more and other than a representation of things (because it "opens access to meanings"). Language, then, is communal and not just personal: we speak to and with one another; and even when we talk to ourselves this is modelled on how we talk to and with others. It not only describes the world but endows it with meaning: it is inescapably tied up with our purposes, and these have not only empirical but also normative significance.

From this perspective, understanding political values and institutions involves what I call "embedded political theory": judgments about the appropriate character of our social bonds that articulate necessary and possible purposes and actions, both individual and collective. It is "political theory" because of its normative quality in exploring what is appropriate for human beings. It is "embedded" because it is located in the understandings we have about who we are and how we should be together, with such understandings forming the core of our values, norms, practices and institutions.

This notion builds on the view of language as something lived through, as something decisive for our having perceptible and recognizable experiences. It assumes that political concepts do not merely shape an external account of political institutions, a description of how these "work" such that the terms of description bear only an accidental connection to the meaningful patterns of activity which define an institution. Concepts form part of our institutions. They help constitute them.

Applied to an account of political and social institutions, the claim that concepts have and constitute reality suggests an idea, "objective spirit," developed by the nineteenth-century German philosopher, G.W.F. Hegel, in his *Philosophy of Right*. Objective spirit referred to the living and lived reality of institutions. As Vincent Descombes explains it, objective spirit means that "social phenomena are intellectual phenomena, and that institutions rest upon representations which are those of the society as such, rather than of associated individuals.... In other words, institutions "think".... [S]ocial life is not reducible to the necessities of common life (utilitarian naturalism), but ... has meaning, and ... individuals derive meaning from it. Meaning is not locked up with the individuals' inner realm; public and collective forms of existence are its natural element."[4]

In other words, social and political institutions are not "things." They are patterned interactions or practices, and they embody and give life to ideas. These ideas could not exist apart from institutions, but institutions would lack sense, indeed wouldn't be recognizable sets of practices at all, without them. In short, institutions as patterned interactions can certainly be described, but as embodiments of ideas, they also and necessarily convey meaning. And such meanings are not just "utilitarian," not just about getting things done, but give shape to what people see as valuable. As an example, I return the issue of voting.[5] In a liberal democratic political system and society with representative institutions, voting is the way in which collective decisions are made. This of course involves putting a mark beside a name on a ballot and adding up all of the marks to determine an outcome. This process involves facts that can be described, as generations of voting studies in political science can attest. But it also has normative meaning as a legitimate way to make a social decision, one potentially binding on everyone. To be "unelected" is a mark of opprobrium, to lack legitimacy, at least most of the time. Such normative significance does not exist apart from the practice of voting as if the act of voting, itself, were just a physical exercise, with the normative judgment tacked on. Rather, the normative dimension constitutes voting as a recognizable practice—it allows us to distinguish this practice as something called "voting," from some other activity where people put a mark on a piece of paper or pull a lever on a machine.

Moreover, voting presupposes you *can* make a social decision by adding up individual votes, the choices of people acting alone, one by one in the voting booth. Other cultures might find this practice puzzling or even unacceptable, believing that social decisions can only be reached by some form of participatory consensus or else they're not social decisions at all. The discussions earlier in this book of the periodic dissatisfaction with representative institutions in our own society, even given the widespread legitimacy voting typically enjoys, illuminates with particular clarity how voting is not just empirical but also normative and indeed that it cannot be properly appreciated unless it is seen as both at the same time.

Individuals never just stand alone. To have an identity as an individual is to participate in a form of collective life that provides terms by which people come to understand themselves in certain ways—including as self-contained individuals.[6] To take a more mundane example than that of voting: many people in our culture are fans of professional sports teams.

Being a fan is to be sure a fact about some individual person, it is meaningful for that individual considered apart from others. I can have my own way of being a fan and can recognize this as an important part of my identity, a "fact" about me, and it may even be more important to who I am than being a voter (I suspect this is true of large numbers of people). At the same time, part of the character of being a fan is that it is a shared experience. Being a fan is usually more than just a fact about someone. A full sense of it involves sharing one's experiences, observations and judgments with others, perhaps by calling a sports 'phone-in' show on the radio or having a conversation with a neighbour across the back fence or meeting a buddy for a beer ("Say, isn't Brett Favre some kind of quarterback? Did you see him throw that touchdown pass while lying on his back!"; "When will the Leafs/Blue Jays/Roughriders dump that bum of a coach/manager?"; and so on). You might say that, in this respect, being a fan is a mediate common good.

Beyond this, when someone is a fan in our society, this involves attachment to a sports enterprise with a history that is in turn part of a larger history—that of professional sports. This latter history possesses a certain social character within which being a fan makes sense. At one level, this involves our understanding, as fans, of the (noble?) history of the team and its competitive performances: a fan of the New York Yankees or of the Montreal Canadians draws upon a long-standing tradition of success so that he/she assesses players today in light of a Babe Ruth or a Joe DiMaggio, a Rocket Richard or a Jean Beliveau, considers the significance of today's club in light of the accomplishments of yesteryear. (Of course, success need not be the only measure here: consider the cases of the Chicago Cubs, or the Boston Red Sox, or the Toronto Maple Leafs.) Here, being a fan partakes something of the character of an immediate common good: the Yankees as the locus of an ongoing practice with shared meanings, valued for its own sake.

On the other hand, professional sports teams are typically profit-seeking enterprises in a capitalist economy, which means they can be understood in the language of political economy. So, for example, professional leagues have a role in generating economic activity (particularly given their currently extensive association with the mass media both in terms of ownership and product) and in purveying capitalist market values. The fan is, in this context at least, partly a construct of the political-economic institutions: he/she is a consumer of entertainment products (and this has always been so, romantic notions of a past when professional sports were supposedly "pure" notwithstanding). Apart from any contemporary economic function, professional sports form part of the history of capitalism and the way in which it became the dominant form of social and economic organization, especially in North America. Sport has its roots in the nineteenth century, as the rapid development of an increasingly urban and industrial capitalism in the U.S. and Canada produced wrenching social change and social conflict. The emergence of the culture of modern sport went along with the attempt to integrate into capitalist society a (predominantly male) working class that was both growing in size and occasionally inclined to radical political behaviour. Sport was seen to combine a model of cooperation, teamwork and the need to accept authority with socially acceptable forms of diversion. Viewed against this history, the fan is someone who displays the vigour of active citizen commitment in a non-civic (and therefore less "dangerous") setting.

"Fan" is an abbreviation of "fanatic," so there is a social-psychological dimension to it. This, too, is rooted in various norms and practices that have emerged over time, from those which determine socially acceptable ways of expressing certain desires to the presence or absence of different ways of achieving gratification and fulfillment, and even to patterns of gender relations and the "codes" or norms that govern what it means to be male or female.[7]

The point here is that qualities we see ourselves as having individually are shaped by our participation in a form of collective life and become understandable in light of the cultural means available for becoming individuals.[8] Thus, where institutions embody objective spirit, they incorporate in recognizable ways important human purposes and provide individual recognition and affirmation. In contrast to the neo-liberal view, the idea here is that institutions are more than regular patterns of activity. They also hold meaning. (Of course they can fail to do so. They can become lifeless, "spiritless." This is the phenomenon social theorists call "alienation.") Where it exists, such meaning involves not only formal limits on our behaviour or the capacity of institutions to provide desired things, to "deliver the goods" (the neo-liberal position). It is also the fulfillment of our identities.

In modern cultures, identity is linked to freedom. In Hegel's view, our freedom is not pre-political or pre-social. It is not a feature of individuals in a "state of nature." It exists only in and through institutions. Institutions should not, therefore, be viewed as unfortunate, if necessary, limitations on our freedom. Nor should they be seen as facilitating a freedom otherwise existing apart from them. They should rather be understood as *expressions* of freedom, as constitutive of a free way of life.

That this is the case can, from Hegel's point of view, be seen when we consider how we engage others in the world on the basis of who we are as individuals, or, to use Hegel's term, "persons." When we think and act, it is always in terms of a particular situation, be this one in our personal/private or in our public/social lives. These situations inescapably involve us with others. The characteristic ways we understand our situations—as worker, lover, consumer, parent, daughter, voter, etc., in short, the content of our identity—do not simply spring from us alone. Our identities are generated together through a process of mutual recognition. The terms of recognition are situationally embedded: they always emerge in contexts where we interact with others. Since our freedom is tied to the achievement of our purposes and our purposes are intertwined with our identities, freedom is therefore something realized not apart from others but with them. In other words, it is realized through institutions and the norms and practices associated with these. For Hegel, humans ultimately had to be citizens of a well-ordered state if they were fully to achieve freedom.[9]

From this perspective, if radical conceptions of individualism and instrumental views of social and political institutions become overwhelmingly dominant and decisive for how we relate to ourselves and others—*in other words, if neo-liberalism becomes "true"*—this would not simply be a fact about us to be noted and accepted. It would entail, rather, a dilemma, a contradiction, a problem. The problem lies in that it is impossible to establish a society on purely individualist grounds alone. The literal attempt to do so—and this is what the elevation and celebration of the market involves—results in a denial of important things about us, and these continue to assert themselves in the face of attempts to will them away.

At the core of this book is the view that such matters are not just esoteric questions of philosophy but go to the heart of urgent public concerns. The tax studies examined in Chapters Two and Three are meaningful and significant because of the ways in which they necessarily confront, by virtue of the logic informing them, the conceptual issues raised here. They are, in other words, expressions of embedded political theory. They are policy documents that are about more than just policy. They open up the question of the nature of polity and society: what these are and where they are going. And they do so because of what taxation means in our political culture: a fundamental expression of our collective commitments and obligations which, in a society at least nominally democratic, must in some sense be self-undertaken and self-imposed. Questions of taxation go to the heart of the issue of how a political community is possible in a civil society in which the generation of material wealth and the sense of individualism typically tied up with this are decisive realities.

Thus, in any explanation of the nature of taxation arrangements and the logic informing these, the question of democracy and its relation to capitalism is never far away. Individual wellbeing, the production of wealth with which such wellbeing is intimately tied, the nature of communal bonds and the place of collective provisioning intersect in complex ways. This intersection defines the terrain of democratic possibilities. In societies both politically democratic and economically capitalist, the answer to the question posed by the classical Greek thinker, Aristotle, "what is a citizen" is, in large part, "one who pays taxes and has a role in selecting the government which levies them." Taxation straddles the divide separating the "private" individual enmeshed in the relation and demands of a capitalist market economy, who in no small measure is defined by what he or she owns, and the "public" citizen-voter sharing in the exercise of formal political power. In a contemporary society such as Canada, democracy is necessarily and fundamentally (although not, of course, exclusively) about how individuals carrying out economic roles are able to come together in a shared community of purpose.

These roles have a class character. The core (although certainly not the only) division in a capitalist society is the class division between owners and non-owners of capital, or means of production, that is, the factories, machines, natural resources and so on which allow the production of goods and services to take place. Cutting through the complexities of specific tax models and debates, the essential question in taxation policy is the allocation of the tax load between those who earn their income from paid employment and those who derive their income from the ownership of wealth, that is, assets which represent claims, rooted in the ownership of capital, on what is produced. The class basis of a capitalist society and how class issues shape the nature and prospects of democracy are two themes the embedded political theory of tax studies helps illuminate.[10]

The issue of class raises the question of inequality—social, economic and political—and its roots in the structures of society, specifically its property relations, those legal forms which establish who owns what and what they are entitled to do with it, particularly if what is owned is capital. Ownership, as the saying goes, has its privileges, and in a capitalist market society these are considerable. This is because, while everyone in a capitalist society "owns" something, if only one's person and its qualities, especially the ability to work, and is entitled to dispose of it as one sees fit within the limits of the law, an owner of capital has the right to employ or not employ people. Since the large majority of people depend upon paid employment for their livelihoods, this gives owners of capital enormous power. Ownership establishes hierarchy in a society that, at least in principle, is supposed to be egalitarian. And this is all legal, all within the rights of private property.

Leo Panitch, a Canadian political scientist and political economist, has written extensively and insightfully about economic and political power, the central place of class and class questions, and the role of the state in Canadian society.[11] Through his work, he has sought to develop a critical account of Canadian society, much of it indebted to the work of Karl Marx and to Marxist theory and scholarship generally, that would contribute to moving Canada toward a more democratic and egalitarian social order. In this context, he has offered an instructive account of taxation in light of class issues and in particular the relation between egalitarian social values and inegalitarian social realities.[12] He argues that "fairness" has long been a commonly held goal of tax policy; even given their differences, both the McLeod and Vicq reports identified it as a key question. However, "fairness" lacks normative insight and depth in light of the issues raised by the relation of taxation to the state. Panitch claims that by themselves notions of "fair taxation" fail either to identify properly the nature of tax equity and what must be done to achieve it or to illuminate fully why tax policy has in recent years emphasized efficiency at the expense of equity. According to him, taxation issues must be addressed in light of the power of capitalists to determine the distribution and use of society's productive resources and hence the boundaries of state action. This is because the ability to determine what will be produced, or if it will be produced at all, affects the resources available to the state as revenue for carrying out its purposes. Under capitalism, the public sector relies primarily on the private sector; the state is embedded in the market.

Hence, the existing relation between the liberal democratic state and the capitalist economy always limits "fair" taxation. Genuine equity can be achieved only through a change in this relationship. This requires a greater focus on the determinants of wealth, income and power—that is, the rights of private property in the means of production—than is typically found in policy debates or in scholarly literature.

This analysis raises fundamental issues and has considerable merit. However, it requires modification on two key points. The first of these involves the need to develop a notion of class that takes more fully into account the complex character of inequality in contemporary society, while maintaining class as an essential basis for confronting the tax question. (Panitch himself has attempted to do this in other, subsequent, work not specifically related to the tax question.) The second point involves linking the dimensions of social and individual life raised by the class question to the idea of embedded political theory and hence the kind of thinking people are called upon to pursue as members of a contemporary liberal democratic and capitalist society.

In recent years, feminist and anti-racist thinkers have mounted radical and challenging criticisms both of society and of political and social theory, including those theories that claim to be critical and progressive. I noted earlier that structural inequalities in a liberal democratic, capitalist society had gendered, racial and ethnic dimensions, that people stood in different relations to the state and the economy. Feminist and anti-racist thinkers and activists have pointed out that conceptions of class, even radical ones, miss forms of domination and stratification not specifically tied to society's property relations, its relations of ownership, although clearly connected to them. Given that, historically, access to paid employment and to property has overwhelmingly been the preserve of European males, with women and racial and ethnic minorities largely marginalized, the concept of class suffers from a blind spot. This is true whether class is thought of as a radical weapon for bringing about fundamental social change or as one way (among others) of describing an existing social order.

Radical or socialist notions of class have traditionally emphasized class as an "objective" attribute of the society because it emerges as a core component of a social structure that forms people and shapes their behaviour. Because class enshrines and maintains the inequality that is seen to thwart the ability of most people to live to their fullest potential, radical and socialist thinkers and activists have generally argued that unequal classes have to be done away with if society is to be fully democratic. The point, then, is that class is not simply a concept to describe how things work, but rather, is central to social transformation. By identifying the structural basis of inequality, the concept functions as a tool that allows people to think differently and critically about their society. Since the majority of people are seen as belonging to the working class—the class under capitalism that lacks ownership of the means of production—this group has normally been viewed as the force in society most in need of, and most likely to pursue, fundamental social change.[13] (This is Leo Panitch's perspective on class, one I tend to share.)

By contrast, more conventional social science treatments of class typically form part of an account of what is called social stratification: patterns of hierarchy and status that have a specific character in an advanced, industrial capitalist society but exist in any social order in that they tend to support tasks or functions required for the society to exist. Such accounts tend to be both descriptive—a component of a social "map" usually defined in terms of income levels, education and occupation, among other characteristics, and rarely linked to a critique of society—and subjective—frequently based on survey data where individuals are asked to describe themselves and their place in the social order. While such accounts can be part of a critical social and political theory, and they can certainly provide important insights into the social order, they are not as likely to be used in this way.[14]

Regardless of whether class is treated descriptively or critically, from the perspective of feminist and anti-racist thinkers, it remains primarily about white males. Class analysis must, therefore, be supplemented by the recognition of the patriarchal, that is, male-dominated, character of society and by the ways in which racial and ethnic identities are created in the culture and become inscribed in the institutions of society as marks of inferiority.[15] This would not only bring to the fore the complex ways in which inequality exists in contemporary society, it would also provide a truer account of how individuals come to have the motives and aspirations they have (or might have) than class analysis could offer by itself.

The American feminist social theorist, Nancy Fraser, has suggested an approach of this kind. She argues that in contemporary society, thinkers and activists must consider questions relating to two kinds of injustice: socioeconomic injustice and cultural or symbolic injustice. She relates these in turn to two kinds of struggle for social change: for redistribution and for recognition. Struggles for redistribution address "socioeconomic injustice, which is rooted in the political-economic structure of society.... Examples include exploitation (having the fruits of one's labor appropriated for the benefit of others); economic marginalization (being confined to undesirable or poorly paid work or being denied access to income-generating labor altogether), and deprivation (being denied an adequate material standard of living)." On the other hand, struggles for recognition address cultural or symbolic injustice. "Here injustice is rooted in social patterns of representation, interpretation, and communication. Examples include cultural domination (being subjected to patterns of interpretation and communication that are associated with another culture and are alien and/or hostile to one's own); nonrecognition (being rendered invisible by means of the authoritative representational, communicative, and interpretative practices of one's culture); and disrespect (being routinely maligned or disparaged in stereotypic public cultural representations and/or in everyday life interactions)."[16]

Such arguments enrich our appreciation of the dimensions and dilemmas of social life and caution us against relying on any single basis for both understanding society and achieving worthwhile social and political aims. Yet, it is also interesting to note that much of the opposition to tax cuts, and neo-liberalism in general, has come from women's organizations and groups speaking on behalf of minorities (as was evident during the hearings of the Vicq Committee). A rational-choice analyst might view this as an expression of self-interest by those who have benefitted most from government programs in relation to the taxes they have paid. But it is just as plausible that women and minorities are more likely than the very powerful to see the world from a less individualistic, more collectivist perspective, and thus on the whole to be less hostile to taxation (even though in certain circumstances they may be more heavily taxed than those who are better off). For while individualism is pervasive in the culture as a whole, the wealthy and powerful are the ones most likely to embrace it and to view it as an inescapable reality. This is why taxation tends to be a "problem" more for them than it typically is for others, even though they are the ones who can afford to pay the taxes. They believe they do not need the public provisioning taxation makes possible.

Even as marginalized groups confront the tax question from the perspective of their specific identities, they also do so in class terms. This is unavoidable. Thus, while the criticisms of class analysis must be acknowledged, the treatment of tax issues must at least be class-weighted. But while acknowledging the significance of class for exploring the meaning of taxation and tax policy, from the point of view of embedded political theory, this cannot be the end of the matter. In relation to taxation, class opens up, in a particularly powerful way, issues of the individual and the community. But it opens them up; it doesn't close them down. It is a start, not an end in itself, a way of getting people to reflect on their personal and social situations. This is the second point of departure from Panitch's account.

This book has focused on the language of policy analysis and what this tells us about explicit and implicit value commitments at work in the culture at different points in time; hence the notion of "embedded political theory." I have argued that this is essential for grasping the range of political possibilities available to social actors in different social and historical contexts.

Leo Panitch, too, defends the need to understand political language, to grasp, for example, "what meaning might be attributed to the rather ambiguous notion of fair taxation." But for him, in the final analysis, "values are only a guide to the action that makes them effective."[17] This conception of the relation of ideas to action, to practice, is too instrumental. It suggests that ideas could be grasped and applied to our practices in a mechanical fashion. But ideas, or values, cannot be set so apart from the practices from which they are derived and to which they give meaning. Thus the approach I adopt is hermeneutic, or interpretative. It holds that our practices are "embodied" ideas, which in turn we understand *as* practices of a recognizably human sort; conversely, no values that have real content can make any sort of sense outside of some practice from which they necessarily receive their meaning. The examples of voting and the nature of the "fan" illustrate this. Both are practices that can be described from the "outside," as it were, that is, as human activities with observable properties. But they are constituted by what is "inside": their meanings as these involve choices about normatively significant wants, needs and purposes. People engaged in these practices are not just doing them; they are expressing something meaningful and relevant to "who" they are. They are interpretations, which can only be fully grasped interpretively.[18]

An interpretive or hermeneutic approach—and this is what the idea of embedded political theory is meant to convey—explores the commitments that might be associated with certain understandings of political reality. It could identify a tension between the aspirations people self-consciously or otherwise exhibit in their motives and actions, and the terms available to them for making sense of their situations. For example, it can explore how the desire of people for community conflicts with currently prevalent individualist, neo-liberal claims about government and taxation.

The idea that there is a tension between what people seek to achieve and what they are called upon to think and do by dominant cultural norms and practices is a central issue in a critical interpretive or hermeneutic approach to political questions. Clarifying the terms by means of which individuals understand themselves could provide them the opportunity to explore alternative ways of relating more coherently and satisfactorily their purposes and activities. No systematic and "rational" account of inequality and exploitation will take hold in the absence, on the part of those who might be persuaded by such an account, of a self-conscious grasp of the meanings and consequences associated with having a certain identity. Simply put, unless people recognize the significance of such an account for both understanding their society and understanding themselves and have some sense the ideas associated with it can make both society and their lives more fulfilling—and that as individuals they can act on them and in fact may already be doing so—they will not respond to it. This awareness is the practical counterpart to embedded political theory, the ideas which constitute our norms, practices and institutions. We "make sense" together, but some forms of this "common" sense are more sensible than others. The task of thinking critically about our situation requires trying to distinguish the more from the less "sensible."

Because of the meaning they hold in the political cultures of liberal democratic states, taxation questions necessarily raise the issue of common-sense, shared understandings about the community and the individual. As the two studies examined here demonstrate, such understandings can change. Different ones may come into conflict with each other. Some may rise, then fall, in importance—then rise again.

The analysis of the studies also shows something else. It indicates that social meanings are the outcome of constant negotiation, that there is no final settlement of issues involving the relation of self to other, individual to community. The idea at the core of certain traditional socialist doctrines, that the self and the collective could and should merge so that there would be no tension between individual purposes and communal goals—that there can be a "general will" that everyone would simply in utter harmony affirm—must be rejected. There will always be an element of imposition in the ways in which individuals confront the demands of their lives together. But these demands could be made more transparent. The means for achieving them could be rendered more accountable and sensitive to the need for people to have self-directed private lives, as well as opportunities for public engagement. Concerns of this sort seem to be crucial to understanding the current dissatisfaction with representative democratic institutions.

The state, or something like it, will always be necessary. Taxation, by which the requirements of collective material provisioning are expressed and carried out, is unavoidable. Put otherwise, in any conceivable political order, including one more egalitarian than existing capitalist liberal democracies, individuals will have to deal with the issue of what is "mine" as opposed to what is "ours." And this has consequences for the range of possible arguments than can be advanced to support critical thinking about the present situation and the need for more egalitarian social and political institutions. It has consequences for democratic theory, particularly progressive or radical forms of it.

Chapter One identified two ways of opening up a critical discussion of democracy in the context of the issues raised in this study: 1) C.B Macpherson's distinction between democracy as a mechanism for choosing and authorizing governments, and democracy as a kind of society dedicated to the equal realization by all of their human capacities (implicitly this also raises the distinction between representative and participatory democratic forms); and 2) John Dryzek's claim that three criteria—franchise, scope and authenticity—allow for an evaluation of existing democratic institutions and of proposals for expanding democratic practices. The positions of both Macpherson and Dryzek make clear that questions about the range and scope of democracy are also necessarily questions about the range and scope of politics itself—that is, the nature of community. The argument in this book is that the examination of the language of the tax studies and the elaboration of embedded political theory as an approach allow us to appreciate this connection. I argue that neo-liberal, market-driven conceptions of the individual and the polity are insufficiently attuned to the role of language and cultural norms in the formation of individual identities and to the unavoidability of community. There is more to experience than calculation at the margin, more than "rational choice."

At the same time, what might be called traditional Marxist, or socialist, criticisms of capitalism and market rationality, and the conception of democracy and community these support, are insufficiently attuned to the tension between self and other, "mine" and "thine." Karl Marx and Friedrich Engels understood political power as the organized force of one class dominating and oppressing another. A radically democratic, that is, socialist or communist, society would do away with classes and thus the need for organized political power. Engels famously, if ambiguously, labelled this process the withering away of the state.[19] This idea exerted tremendous influence on subsequent generations of Marxists. Whether the disappearance of the *state* meant the disappearance of *politics* as the expression and reconciliation of social differences and competing social goals was left unclear. Certainly the idea of a trouble-free, frictionless, harmonious society has been a powerful current within modern societies, and Marxists have not been the only ones to embrace it. Indeed, liberalism, and most especially neo-liberalism, has always seemed suspicious of conflict as a harbinger of unsettling social change and hostile to the state and public life as potentially threatening to self-contained, "free" individuals. Not only Marxists have wanted to replace "the government of persons by the administration of things"; indeed, the modern bureaucratic state emerged within capitalist society.[20]

The notion of a fully harmonious community expressing a common or general will has played a significant role in much socialist thinking about democracy. Marx and Engels (especially the latter) assumed that class, rooted in society's relations of material production, was the overwhelmingly fundamental, if not sole, source of domination in capitalist society. Eliminating the economic basis of domination would at the same time eliminate the need for political power in the service of this or in response to the conflicts it generated. But as earlier noted, both the history of modern societies and the ideas of feminist and anti-racist thinkers and activists have made clear that there are other forms of domination and social conflict that can't be reduced to those involving class, narrowly interpreted. Indeed, it may be that the emergence of alternative conceptions of social differences and social struggle reflected and reinforced the insight that, while the state could be transformed, as a setting for politics it could not be done away with.

On the other hand, as Fraser's position suggests, such non-class differences are not only a basis for domination but, potentially at least, positive expressions of human diversity and human flourishing. Since a fully egalitarian and democratic community would necessarily be about this, politics as a practice concerned with the affairs of the community would be an essential ingredient of the positive expression of difference. To use the older, classical Aristotelian view of the matter, politics would be about the good life. (Something like this also resonates with a republican model of citizenship and the state.) Whether viewed from the perspective of multiple sources of domination and struggle or on the basis of the need to ensure that differences are acknowledged, respected and promoted, the problems posed by the traditional Marxist or socialist conceptions of democracy, and the responses to them, indicate that community and solidarity are never fully and finally achieved but require ongoing negotiation.[21]

Recently, another kind of democratic theory, deliberative democracy, has come to prominence. Deliberative democracy offers a way of addressing the limits of other accounts of democracy because of two characteristics in particular. First, it seems to have a natural affinity with a political analysis based on language and embedded assumptions. Second, the fact that it refers to deliberation implies the need for the negotiation and expression of differences in the course of making collective decisions.

At the core of deliberative democracy is "the idea that legitimate lawmaking issues from the public deliberation of citizens. As a normative account of legitimacy, deliberative democracy evokes ideals of rational legislation, participatory politics, and civic self-governance."[22] (In this respect it evokes echoes of the republican model of politics.) The theory assumes that all those affected by a political decision are entitled to participate equally in an authentic process of deliberation, which would result in decisions based on rational judgment, the force of the better argument. This model of deliberative democracy both addresses the issues raised by Macpherson and Dryzek and serves as an alternative to both neoliberal and classical socialist conceptions of democracy. It presumes more than self-interested individual choice and also rejects the idea of an integral community that would not need to deliberate but simply give voice to its common will. It is, in short, a way of connecting "democracy" with "difference."[23] It suggests that it is possible to achieve communicatively a form of solidarity, that is, social and political ties that are more than instrumental. In offering a view of democracy as a set of deliberative procedures, open equally to all, deliberative democrats defend the idea that it is possible to achieve substantive common purposes without falling prey to the dangerously utopian aspiration for a community founded upon a single, "true" way of life for all.

There is much that is worthwhile in this. But as this brief account of deliberative democracy suggests, although it purports to be based on values and practices that can be found in existing liberal democratic societies (particularly the United States), the theory has the quality of an ideal-type model, a set of desirable principles, and it has been criticized on these grounds. Critics have pointed to the difficulty, if not impossibility, of attaining this ideal in a society of structured inequalities, where people lack resources, opportunities and encouragement, where their (prospectively) deliberative "voices" are muted or silenced altogether?[24] (All public issues can be treated in a way that excludes significant elements of the population; tax questions especially so, both because in an unequal society they are at the heart of things and because they are so often defined as "technical.") At the same time, the very notion of rational deliberation gives pride of place to "conventional" and "respectable" forms of argumentation and presentation, to the exclusion of processes of communication that are "far more rowdy, disorderly, and decentered," including "tactics such as strikes, boycotts, and disruptive demonstrations."[25] Such "non-normal" forms of communication are of course typically deployed by the marginal and excluded as means of pressuring authorities to respond to their needs and interests; hence criticisms of deliberative democracy on these grounds reflect the feminist and anti-racist concerns discussed earlier in this chapter. Critics such as Iris Marion Young do not disavow rational discourse, "a willingness to give reasons for one's claims and listen to others ... articulate reasonable appeals to justice," but argue that participants in "democratic communication" should also be able to "expose the sources and consequences of structural inequalities in law, the hegemonic terms of discourse, and the environment of everyday practice."[26] In short, democratic theory needs to be both "deliberative" and "activist."

Debates around deliberative democracy, especially as these have been broadened out by criticisms of the sort noted here, are useful and suggestive. They open up issues of participatory versus representative democracy and of democracy as a form of government versus democracy as a kind of society. They also advance discussion about the issues of franchise (who participates and how), scope (the nature of the issues dealt with) and authenticity (whether all are included under terms which permit real participation about issues vital to individual and social wellbeing). Yet, whether one emphasizes "rational," ordered (likely institutionalized) discussion or more "non-conventional" communicative forms, there remains the question posed in Chapter One and carried throughout this book: "To what extent can my purposes be fulfilled only together with others; indeed, to what extent are my purposes *our* purposes, defined by being shared, and not just mine alone?" Deliberative democratic theory is on the right track with its focus on language, but the "legitimate-ness" of outcomes of deliberative processes (conventional or unconventional) seems obscure. Democratic legitimacy has to link up with fundamental questions of value and human aspiration, of the sort entailed by the notion of embedded political theory. As the great eighteenth-century political theorist (and democrat) Jean-Jacques Rousseau might have put it, the issue has to be put in the right way, in the circumstances we actually confront.[27] And, in my view, the circumstances today still require that a democratic political theory explicitly articulate the relation of capitalism to democracy, something that most theorists of deliberative democracy do not do. This is not because invoking these terms somehow magically alters the world of either theory or practice, as if they had magus-like properties. Rather, they help us get a fuller sense of what is at stake in terms of the range of human qualities at play in contemporary society and hence a richer grasp on what matters to us as individuals who also are called upon to share our lives together.

In light of this, I want to return to the democratic theory of C.B. Macpherson. His ideas can more fully illuminate the meaning and significance of taxation for a democratic political order. They provide a fitting conclusion to this chapter. In his *Life and Times of Liberal Democracy*, originally published in 1977, Macpherson examined a form of democracy he called the "pluralist, elitist, equilibrium" model. "It is pluralist in that it starts from the assumption that the society which a modern democratic political system must fit is a plural society, that is, a society consisting of individuals each of whom is pulled in many directions by his [sic] many interests, now in company with one group of his fellows, now with another. It is elitist in that it assigns the main role in the political process to self-chosen groups of leaders. It is an equilibrium model in that it presents the democratic process as a system which maintains an equilibrium between the demand and supply of political goods."[28]

In this model, democracy is seen as a market-like mechanism. A democratic political system aggregates the preferences of citizens who are understood as political "consumers" enjoying "consumer sovereignty." With its roots in the powerful utilitarian tradition and in neo-classical microeconomic theory, the model claims to be a realistic account of how people actually behave. It professes to be "scientific"; it can be empirically verified. By contrast, other accounts of democracy are considered either unscientific or "ideological," by which is meant, roughly, "radical" or "socialist," and thus empirically and morally suspect. Writing in the nineteen sixties and seventies, Macpherson thought the pluralist, elitist, equilibrium model was the then dominant account of democracy, both academically in the university and ideologically in the larger society. In the form of the "public choice" account of political decisionmaking, it still is.[29]

Macpherson attributed the success of this model to its having emerged primarily during the post-war era in advanced and expanding consumer capitalist societies, such as the United States. He wondered whether it would hold up should economic growth slacken or become more uncertain. (It seems to have done so.) But, while tied to the achievement of high levels of economic growth and indeed justifying itself on the basis of the ability of the political and economic systems to "deliver the goods," the pluralist, elitist, equilibrium model of democracy does something else. It sustains a certain view of human nature and a specific social structure. The view of human nature is that individuals are essentially consumers, appropriators of goods, services and capital. The social structure is one characterized by extensive, class-based inequalities. According to Macpherson, these characteristics substantially diminish the democratic content of both the model and the society it explains and justifies. They make it difficult, if not impossible, for large numbers of people to participate effectively in the democratic process, while at the same time allowing a relative few with considerable resources of money and time and a sense of political efficacy to disproportionately shape political outcomes.

Earlier noted, Macpherson favoured a much more egalitarian society. Such a society would be one in which individuals saw themselves not so much as consumers and appropriators (as "market man," to use Macpherson's terminology) but rather as doers and exerters of their distinctively human capacities. He believed this would incline people away from the ruthless competition of a capitalist market social order and toward greater cooperation. Were this to occur, democracy would then no longer be seen only as a mechanism for choosing and authorizing governments, or as a vehicle for aggregating "public choices." It would then be a kind of society in which individuals were equally able to use and develop their capacities.[30]

The achievement of such a society would require dramatic political, economic and social change, ultimately a popular political movement on behalf of equality. In his typically spare and understated style, Macpherson simply but profoundly identified a key element shaping and limiting the range of meaningful and plausible political possibilities available to individuals in an advanced capitalist society. The pluralist, elitist, equilibrium conception of democracy would remain "the most accurate descriptive model, and ... continue to be accepted as an adequate justificatory model, *as long as we in Western societies continue to prefer affluence to community (and to believe that the market society can provide affluence indefinitely)*.[31]

By "affluence," Macpherson understood the form of material prosperity linked to the acquisitive behaviour of individuals in an advanced capitalist society.[32] This involves a wellbeing gained through successful competitive struggle with others; indeed it is defined in terms of such success. The struggle is at the heart of a market liberalism, understood as the "freedom of the stronger to do down the weaker by following market rules."[33] It is this liberalism, with its commitment to market freedoms, competition and private gain, that informs the neo-liberal paradigm.

For Macpherson, the preference for market-driven affluence had a cost. The cost was the absence of community and solidarity sustained by a liberalism identified, not with ruthless market competition, but rather with the "equal, effective freedom of all to use and develop their capacities."[34] Macpherson's value judgment was that people would be happier and more fulfilled in an egalitarian, solidaristic social order than in an unequal, competitive one.

This is a powerful claim. But for this to happen—that is, for class-based inequalities to become an explicit and serious question in liberal democratic states formally committed to equality—it is essential to deal with two dimensions of the relation between capitalism and democracy that help sustain a widespread preference for affluence over community. First, the formal political rights available in a liberal (capitalist) democracy—the right to vote and form political parties, as well as freedoms of speech and association—permit only in a limited sense those disadvantaged by the relations of power in the society to organize in support of social change. Although these rights remain justifiably highly valued, they have unequal weight in practice because of material inequalities—the fact, for example, that trade unions have far fewer resources to make their voices heard and their views prevail than do corporations.

The second dimension that needs to change has to do with Macpherson's view of human nature in a capitalist market society and the penchant of individuals to see themselves as acquirers and appropriators without limit. This dimension involves the ability of a capitalist, liberal democracy to satisfy the very interests it creates and promotes, interests defined in terms of short-term material gain achieved through narrowly defined rational, or instrumental, calculation. This state of affairs reinforces highly individualistic perceptions of how one relates to others in society.[35]

These are major impediments to the radical perspective on democracy that Macpherson promotes. But it is a considerable strength of his analysis that he makes central language—"affluence" versus "community"—within which these dimensions can be clearly brought to light and, at least in principle, made the basis for widespread deliberation about the nature of a vibrant democracy and a good society. So posed, the question of affluence versus community also harbours the possibility of relating class questions to other sources of injustice. Affluence is not neutral in gender or racial terms, while the language of community can permit, and indeed require, reflection about how to include all within the structures and relations of society in ways that more adequately fulfill human aspirations for connectedness.

Macpherson's position fused the critique of capitalism provided by Karl Marx with the ideals of individual self-development defended by the nineteenth-century English liberal political thinker, John Stuart Mill, who was a staunch defender of individual freedom.[36] Macpherson never spelled out fully an account of a solidaristic society of equal individuals no longer constrained by the unequal class relations of a capitalist society. Some critics have thus seen in his position an unrealistic, utopian dream of a fully harmonious society of equal, self-developing individuals, precisely what theorists of deliberative democracy dismiss and what I earlier suggested was a major problem with traditional socialist notions of democracy.[37] But although a proponent of a radically transformed system of democracy, Macpherson never argued for the withering away of the state or the disappearance of the organized political community: he seemed to believe that even in a fully egalitarian democratic society, there would still be political and social differences to resolve. Nor did he think individuals would ever have to stop thinking about, or debating, how as individuals they ought to relate to the larger community. In this respect he never denied there would always be the need for the protection of individual rights, a cornerstone of liberal political ideas.[38]

Viewed in this light, Macpherson's position is not simply utopian speculation but rather possesses a significant dimension of realism. If the hermeneutic approach to political analysis outlined in this book is plausible, then people actually *do* confront in their values and practices something like the dilemma Macpherson identifies. They wrestle with the conflicting pressures of a utilitarian and a developmental understanding of their purposes and motives. It might be that these pressures are even more acute today because neo-liberal ideas and policies so vigorously enjoin us to adopt a predominantly utilitarian outlook. In other words, we are in part *made* to prefer affluence to community. An approach to democracy and taxation that is both more normatively attractive and empirically sound must take this into account.

My primary intention in pursuing as part of the account of embedded political theory this brief examination of contemporary democratic thought, including that of Macpherson, is not to classify and criticize it *per se*. Rather, I want to suggest that how taxation is dealt with in theory and practice illuminates questions of democracy, understood as collective self-government under conditions of equality. In this respect, my argument turns on two claims: 1) democratic tax policy (or any policy) requires deliberation as a setting within which social goals are set; and 2) where deliberation genuinely occurs under conditions whereby people can actually reflect on their bonds (and this doesn't have to mean they are all literally assembled), they will come to a more communal understanding of their situation than neo-liberalism permits. Potentially, deliberative democracy might offer more insight into these matters than does mainstream liberal democratic or classical socialist democratic theory. But the lack of an account of how deliberation links up with actual patterns of social life, especially with respect to issues of political economy and class, limits it. Macpherson's ideas help fill this gap.³⁹

If we remain agnostic about whether Macpherson intended some 'ultimate' solution to the problem of which of the two liberalisms he identifies should prevail, his position can illuminate what is at stake in debates about taxation, because the issue of equity versus efficiency is the expression, at the level of tax policy, of the more fundamental matter Macpherson raises—affluence versus community. This is the issue visible at the level of embedded political theory, the assumptions about human nature, politics and society, which shape perceptions about the kind of social order both desirable and possible. These assumptions can be traced in both the McLeod and Vicq reports; as suggested above, both address the relation of capitalism to democracy. The question of affluence versus community brings deliberations about taxation norms and practices to life, not as the preserve of technical specialists or policy designers but as fundamental concerns of citizens who must find a way to live together by deciding about those things they have to provide for each other.

Notes

1. In a personal interview with me, Dr. Jack Boan, Professor Emeritus of Economics at the University of Regina, who had done work for the McLeod Commission, confirmed this. After the Royal Commission report was released publicly, Premier Thatcher took considerable pains to distance himself from it. To correct the "erroneous impression" that the report represented government policy, he noted that "this royal commission, under the chairmanship of Dean T.H. McLeod, was set up in June 1963, by the former government of this province" and even if the commission had been appointed by his government, "it should perhaps be pointed out that the findings of any such body are nothing more than findings and whatever government receives them is free to act upon them, or not act upon them, as it sees fit." Claiming that in the case of the McLeod report, "perhaps more so than in many" cases, its recommendations should not be viewed in any way as government policy, the Premier also indicated that his government did not agree "with the commission's assumption that the public wants a greater share of its income spent on government services." He also professed to be more optimistic about the economic development prospects for the province than was the Commission. ["Thatcher states taxation report not government policy" *The Leader-Post* (Regina) July 8, 1965, 3.] For an account of the Thatcher government and its impact on Saskatchewan politics, see Dale A. Eisler, *Rumours of Glory: Saskatchewan and the Thatcher Years* (Edmonton: Hurtig, 1987). See also David Smith, *Prairie Liberalism: The Liberal Party in Saskatachewan 1905–71* (Toronto and Buffalo: University of Toronto Press, 1975). It is worth noting that while the Thatcher government pursued what were in the context of the time more conservative policies, to a significant degree it accepted the Keynesian welfare state consensus. One example of this was in the field of housing policy. On this, see Lance Dawson, *Evolution of Social Housing Policy in Saskatchewan: A Comparative Study of Regina and Moose Jaw, 1944-*

1982 (unpublished M.A. Thesis, Department of History, University of Regina, 1996).
2. For evidence of the extent to which the recommendations of the Personal Income Tax Review Committee have been accepted by the provincial government, see Saskatchewan Minister of Finance, *Budget Address*, March 30, 2001.
3. Charles Taylor, "Heidegger, Language and Ecology," in C. Taylor, *Philosophical Arguments* (Cambridge, MA: Harvard University Press, 1995), 112.
4. Vincent Descombes, "Is there an objective spirit?" in James Tully (ed.), *Philosophy in an Age of Pluralism: The Philosophy of Charles Taylor in Question* (Cambridge: Cambridge University Press, 1994), 97.
5. This example draws from Charles Taylor, *Hegel and Modern Society* (Cambridge: Cambridge University Press, 1979), 88ff.
6. Thus, Asher and Gad Horowitz argue that in "the form of society that is modern, capitalist, and bureaucratic—of which the liberal paradigm is the ideological expression—there is a corresponding negative hallucination and suppression of the partness of the individual [i.e., that the individual is part of a larger whole] ... a negative hallucination is not seeing something that is there." Asher Horowitz and Gad Horowitz, "Everywhere They Are in Chains" *Political Theory from Rousseau to Marx* (Scarborough, ON: Nelson, 1988), 2.
7. For an excellent and detailed treatment of the socio-economic, political, ideological and psychological issues posed by the rise of the culture of modern sports, and in particular the construction of gender identities and the forms of social power rooted in these, see Varda Burstyn, *Rites of Men: Manhood, Politics, and the Culture of Sport* (Toronto: University of Toronto Press, 1999).
8. To avoid any misunderstanding: my discussion here is by no means intended as a denunciation of the fan as utterly misguided, a victim of what Marxists have called "false consciousness." Rather, the point is to indicate the complex character of this and other dimensions of personal identity that, like the society from which it emerges, partakes of the good and bad, the authentic and the spurious. For an interesting and somewhat different take on the nature of the fan and professional sports in capitalist society, and their complex character, see Christopher Lasch, *The Culture of Narcissism: American Life in an Age of Diminishing Expectations* (New York: W.W. Norton & Company, 1978), ch.V. For an excellent account of the political economy of professional sports, with reference to the circumstances surrounding the departure of the National Hockey League Winnipeg Jets for Phoenix, AZ, see Jim Silver, *Thin Ice: Money, Politics and the Demise of an NHL Franchise* (Halifax: Fernwood Publishing, 1996). A more comprehensive treatment of the same issues with respect to hockey in Canada is Richard Gruneau and David Whitson, *Hockey Night in Canada: Sports, Identities and Cultural Politics* (Toronto: Garamond Press, 1993). See as well Burstyn, *The Rites of Men*.
9. G.W.F. Hegel, *Elements of the Philosophy of Right* (1820), ed. by Allen W. Wood, trans. by H.B. Nisbet (Cambridge: Cambridge University Press, 1991). Hegel's language and his political thought are notoriously difficult. For a helpful interpretation of his argument, see Kenneth Westphal, "The basic context and structure of Hegel's Philosophy of Right," in Frederick C. Beiser, ed., *The Cambridge Companion to Hegel* (Cambridge: Cambridge University Press, 1993), 234–69.
10. For a detailed empirical and conceptual treatment of the nature and signifi-

cance of class in a number of advanced capitalist countries, see Wallace Clement and John Myles, *Relations of Ruling: Class and Gender in Postindustrial Societies* (Montreal and Kingston: McGill-Queen's University Press, 1994).
11. For an excellent and still valuable discussion of the nature of class both as a concept and in the context of Canadian history and politics, see his "Elites, Classes, and Power in Canada," in Michael S. Whittington and Glen Williams (eds.), *Canadian Politics in the 1990s* Fourth Edition (Scarborough, ON: Nelson, 1995), 152–75.
12. Leo Panitch, "Beyond the Crisis of the Tax State? From Fair Taxation to Structural Reform," in Allan M. Maslove, ed., *Fairness in Taxation: Exploring the Principles* (Toronto: University of Toronto Press, 1993), 135–59.
13. For a classic statement of this position, see Karl Marx and Friedrich Engels, *The Communist Manifesto* (originally written in 1848; this edition, 1888) (New York and Toronto: Bantam Books, 1992). See as well Marx and Engels, *The German Ideology* (1846), particularly the first section, included in David McLellan (ed.), *Karl Marx: Selected Writings* Second Edition (Oxford: Oxford University Press, 2000). For a demanding but insightful critical account of the Marxian concept of class, one sympathetic to its basic aims, see Jean L. Cohen, *Class and Civil Society: The Limits of Marxian Critical Theory* (Amherst, MA: The University of Massachusetts Press, 1982).
14. For a comprehensive treatment of different and alternative theories of class, see Edward G. Grabb, *Theories of Social Inequality: Classical and Contemporary Perspectives* Third Edition (Toronto: Harcourt Brace & Company, 1997). For a more detailed account of class and social stratification along the lines sketched here, one specifically concerned with the Marxian conception, see Frank Parkin, *Marxism and Class Theory: A Bourgeois Critique* (New York: Columbia University Press, 1979).
15. On these issues, see for example, Varda Burstyn, ed., *Women, Class, Family and the State* (Toronto: Garamond Press, 1985); and Nancy C.M. Hartsock, *Money, Sex and Power: Toward a Feminist Historical Materialism* (Boston: Northeastern University Press, 1985). For a contemporary discussion of the issues, with extensive references to the literature, see Leah F. Vosko, "The Pasts (and Futures) of Feminist Political Economy in Canada: Reviving the Debate," *Studies in Political Economy* 68 (Summer 2002), 55–83. A brief review of feminist theory in general, in relation to the role and nature of politics and the state, is Murray Knuttila and Wendee Kubik, *State Theories: Classical, Global and Feminist Perspectives* Third Edition (Halifax & London: Ferwood Publishing/Zed Books, 2000), ch. 9.
16. Nancy Fraser, "From Redistribution to Recognition? Dilemmas of Justice in a 'Postsocialist' Age," in Fraser, *Justice Interruptus: Critical Reflections on the "Postsocialist" Condition* (New York & London: Routledge, 1997), 13, 14. See also her "Heterosexism, Misrecognition, and Capitalism: A Response to Judith Butler," *New Left Review* 1/228 (March-April 1998), 140–9; and "Rethinking Recognition," *New Left Review* 3 (May-June, 2000), 107–21. Vosko, "The Pasts..." discusses the debates surrounding Fraser's position. By "postsocialist" condition, Fraser means the situation following the collapse of the Soviet model of state socialism and the significant weakening, if not disappearance altogether, of the social democratic Keynesian welfare state, both of which justified themselves on the basis of economic equality. In the postsocialist condition,

110 / Taxing Illusions

"group identity supplants class interest as the chief medium of political mobilization. Cultural domination supplants exploitation as the fundamental injustice. And cultural recognition displaces socioeconomic redistribution as the remedy for injustice and the goal of political struggle." (11)

17. Panitch, "Beyond the Crisis of the Tax State?...," 139.
18. Part of the problem we typically have in understanding the nature of interpretation as I've sought to define it is that in our everyday language we are apt to see actions as "out there" in the world, while interpretations appear as purely mental phenomena, things going on in our heads. They are unsupported by "hard" evidence and thus without reality. There is no room to provide here the philosophical justification of my position; a particularly powerful and influential argument in this respect is Charles Taylor, "Interpretation and the Sciences of Man" (1964), in *Philosophy and the Human Sciences,* 15–57. But there are everyday terms that give a hint. For example, we may speak of someone's "body language." This is clearly not intended as a "scientific" statement. It is an interpretation. But we use it as evidence, as having reality, as telling us something we can defend and justify.
19. The core argument can be found in *The Communist Manifesto*. The relevant passage from Engels' work reads: "As soon as there is no longer any social class to be held in subjection; as soon as class rule, and the individual struggle for existence based upon our present anarchy of production, with the collisions and excesses arising from these, are removed, nothing more remains to be repressed, and a special repressive force, a state, is no longer necessary.... State interference in social relations becomes, in one domain after another, superfluous, and then dies out of itself; the government of persons is replaced by the administration of things, and by the conduct of processes of production. The state is not 'abolished.' It dies out." Friedrich Engels, *Socialism: Utopian and Scientific* (originally published 1878; English edition 1892), in Robert C. Tucker *The Marx-Engels Reader* Second Edition (New York: W.W. Norton & Company, 1978), 713. The emphasis is in the original.
20. For an account of the anti-political thrust of much modern political thinking, see Carole Pateman, "Sublimation and Reification: Locke, Wolin and the Liberal Democratic Conception of the Political," *Politics and Society* 15 (1975), 441–67.
21. It should be noted that human flourishing was itself for Marx at the heart of the necessity for the transition to socialism. See, for example relevant passages in *The German Ideology*. For a challenging and insightful account of the philosophical basis of Marx's position on this question, see Carol C. Gould, *Marx's Social Ontology: Individuality and Community in Marx's Theory of Social Reality* (Cambridge, MA, and London: The MIT Press, 1980).
22. James Bohman and William Rehg, eds., *Deliberative Democracy* (Cambridge, MA: The MIT Press, 1997), ix. This is a valuable collection of essays, which offers different perspectives on deliberative democracy, its institutional requirements, its implications for society and the potential problems it could create. See also John S. Dryzek, *Deliberative Democracy: Liberals, Critics, Contestations* (Oxford: Oxford University Press, 2000).
23. Anne Phillips, *Democracy & Difference* (University Park, PA: The Pennsylvania State University Press, 1993).
24. On this point, see Brooke A. Ackerly, *Political Theory and Feminist Social*

"Embedded Political Theory" and Democracy / 111

   Criticism (Cambridge: Cambridge University Press, 2000).
25. Iris Marion Young, "Activist Challenges to Deliberative Democracy," *Political Theory* Vol.29, No.5 (October, 2001), 688, 680. Young adds: "processes of engaged and responsible democratic communication include street demonstrations and sit-ins, musical works, and cartoons, as much as parliamentary speeches and letters to the editor" (688). Unconventional methods are always suspect in the eyes of 'respectable' opinion, as evidenced by the criticisms voiced currently of anti-globalization activists.
26. Ibid., 688.
27. Rousseau, "The Social Contract," in Cole, *The Social Contract and Discourses*, 179–309.
28. C.B. Macpherson, *The Life and Times of Liberal Democracy*, 77.
29. It is worth noting that the heyday of the pluralist, elitist, equilibrium model, as Macpherson understood it, coincided with the triumph of Keynesianism, while its current incarnation has emerged with the ascension of neo-liberalism. If, following Macperson, we assume that models and practices of democracy are historical and tied to the development of capitalism, then it would follow that in spite of the evident differences between Keynesianism and neo-liberalism, the underlying structural social and economic forces at work are similar. This is why, in any exploration of the character and consequences of existing political forms and values, it is essential to go beyond an account of different policy.
30. Macpherson most fully and powerfully developed these themes in *Democratic Theory: Essays in Retrieval*.
31. Macpherson, *The Life and Times...* 91–2. Emphasis added.
32. That Macpherson understood affluence as historically specific was made clear by his view that economic, or distributive, justice, which involves an ethically appropriate distribution of the social product, could, and should, eventually give way. It would be replaced by "a concept of human fulfilment which would surpass the concept of economic justice" and "which may be summed up as quality of life: not merely the quality of the physical environment ... but also the quality of the social and economic institutions which would be seen as determining (and hampering) the chances of the full use and development of human capacities" ["The Rise and Fall of Economic Justice," in C.B. Macpherson, *The Rise and Fall of Economic Justice and Other Essays* (Oxford & New York: Oxford University Press, 1985), 20, 17. Macpherson clearly had in mind here an understanding of human wellbeing different from that linked to capitalist affluence. He tied the disappearance of distributive justice to the overcoming of scarcity, which he believed capitalism had made possible. With enough for all, there would be no need for a principle of allocation, or rationing. This might be thought hopelessly unrealistic. But the normative and even institutional questions raised by Macpherson's position make his claim worthy of serious attention.
33. Macpherson, *The Life and Times...* 1.
34. Ibid.
35. Two American political theorists, Joshua Cohen and Joel Rogers, have identified these two dimensions of the capitalist, liberal democratic experience as, respectively, the "resource constraint" and the "demand constraint." See their lucid treatment of these in their *On Democracy: Toward a Transformation of American Society* (New York: Penguin Books, 1983), esp. 50–67. I am indebted

to Bob Ware for suggesting to me the relevance of these arguments for my discussion here.

36. For an excellent account of the ideas of Marx and Mill, in the broader context of the kinds of issues Macpherson treats and their relation to the main currents of modern political thought, see Andrew Levine, *Engaging Political Philosophy: from Hobbes to Rawls* (Malden, MA: Blackwell Publishers, 2002).

37. For criticisms along these lines, see John Keane, "Stretching the Limits of the Democratic Imagination," in Joseph H. Carens, ed., *Democracy and Possessive Individualism: The Intellectual Legacy of C.B. Macpherson* (Albany, NY: State University of New York Press, 1993), 105–35.

38. Macpherson's own definition of his theoretical project captures these themes: "what I have been trying to do all along ... [is] ... work out a revision of liberal-democratic theory, a revision which clearly owes a good deal to Marx, in the hope of making that theory more democratic while rescuing that valuable part of the liberal tradition which is submerged when liberalism is identified with capitalist market relations." Macpherson, "Humanist Democracy and Elusive Marxism: A Response to Minogue and Svacek," *Canadian Journal of Political Science* IX:3 (September 1976), 423.

39. John Dryzek, who is identified with deliberative democracy, has recently suggested the need for deliberative theory to take into account issues such as those posed by Macpherson. He defends what he calls discursive democracy, by which he means a form of deliberative democracy that is critically oriented toward established structures of power, "including those that operate beneath the constitutional surface of the liberal state." He argues that discursive democracy "should be pluralistic in embracing the necessity to communicate across difference without erasing difference, reflexive in its questioning orientation to established traditions (including the tradition of deliberative democracy itself), transnational in its capacity to extend across state boundaries into settings where there is no constitutional framework, ecological in terms of openness to communication with non-human nature, and dynamic in its openness to ever-changing constraints and opportunities for democratization." As part of this approach, he also indicates that class questions may well have a place; indeed he criticizes Ulrich Beck, one of the main architects of the idea that we now live in an international "risk" society for exaggerating "the degree to which issues of economic growth and material distribution are vanishing." Dryzek, *Delberative Democracy and Beyond*, 2, 3, 165. Dryzek's position here represents a potentially significant deepening of the deliberative framework. However, in my view, Macpherson's argument still captures important concerns about democracy that have not yet found in place in other accounts.

Chapter Six

The "Free" Market, Embedded Political Theory—and Us

As this book is being written (summer/fall 2002), Canada and the United States are undergoing a period of tumult in their financial markets. In the face of the collapse of new technology stocks, massive accounting frauds leading to the bankruptcy of formerly huge enterprises such as the energy trading company, Enron, and the communications giant, WorldCom, and unfavourable earnings statements from a large number of important enterprises, there is the widespread feeling of crisis, of dread. With stock values gyrating wildly in the context of a generally precipitous plunge in the markets and with currency values following suit, there are fears that turmoil in the financial sector will spill over into the "real" economy of productive activity and create an economic downturn, a recession.

On a typical day during the summer of 2002, the Business section of *The Globe and Mail*, which bills itself as Canada's "national" newspaper, reported on the current financial problems and in particular a rapid slide in the value of the Canadian dollar. The report noted that Canada's Minister of Finance, John Manley, attributed the turbulence and uncertainty to the fact that "[m]arkets have their own minds." It also quoted an economist from the Bank of Nova Scotia on why the currency was doing so badly while the "economic fundamentals" of the country seemed to be sound: "The problem is that the currency hasn't reacted, and doesn't want to react, to some of these longer-term fundamentals."[1] Almost daily one can find many examples of this kind of language, in good economic times as well as bad. We rather take it for granted; it hardly seems unusual. But it is.

This way of describing the world is what critical social and political theorists call reification: viewing things and abstractions as if they had human properties of will and motivation—and viewing humans as if they were things.[2] "Markets" and "the currency" are spoken of as if they had consciousness and the capacity to act. But they are abstractions. What are attributed to them are in reality the motives, intentions and actions of human beings. Hence, the outcomes of human activity are seen as if they had spontaneously sprung up, as if they were inescapable facts of nature. If markets and currencies, indeed economic life in general, are facts of nature, there is not much one can do about them. Indeed, to interfere with them is to violate the laws of nature itself, to meddle where we ought not. We should not interfere with "free" markets just as we should not interfere with "free" individuals, and for the same reason: such interference threatens always to violate their integrity, their identity, their dignity.

This book has sought to demonstrate that the language and values of neo-liberalism in particular reflect and contribute to reification.³ This is why one of the hallmarks of neo-liberal discourse is the commonly asserted claim that there is no alternative to the implementation of neo-liberal policy prescriptions. The theorists of reification see this sort of claim as expressing the idea that there is nothing humans can or should do to address the consequences of what they have already done, that we are helpless in the face of our own powers.

In light of this, the language of "the market" has become so prevalent that certain important qualities of this discourse have tended to be overlooked or taken for granted. There is no market as such. As an abstraction, the term is a shorthand or crystallized expression of certain forms of human interaction. So understood, "the market" denotes a pattern of human relations geared to the production and reproduction of the material conditions of social life. This pattern expresses a judgment about what is to be produced, the form this is to assume and the motives shaping the choices about how human energies are to be mobilized. This judgment at the core of the market relation holds that what is produced must be a commodity, that is, something to be bought and sold. Only that which can be bought and sold has value or worth. The motive informing the use of human energies is acquisitiveness: the maximization of wellbeing such that self-interested and self-seeking individuals engage in actions which fulfill potentially limitless preferences. Self-seeking individuals so motivated act independently of the self-seeking actions of others, save insofar as these actions either impede or facilitate the quest for satisfaction of preferences or desires.

Viewed as a form of social organization and not as a thing, the market can not be understood as a fact of nature but rather as the product of human interaction. It thus involves will and choice, which are themselves shaped by social and political relations, and this brings into play authority and power, the capacity to define what is socially valuable and appropriate. Like the Hobbesian state of nature, which is a metaphor for it, the market is a social, not a pre-social or natural condition. The idea that the market is somehow "out there" and not embedded in society is a kind of illusion about how society itself is organized to produce its means of subsistence. The illusion is that social production "somehow happens" as a consequence of the play of natural laws and that human agents are simply vehicles through which these laws are carried out.

This illusion benefits those who actually do make the decisions about the use of social and natural resources and the organization of human energy. In contemporary capitalist societies such as Canada, those who decide are primarily large, profit-driven, private interests. An important basis of the power of such interests to make these decisions, and thus of "the market," is the idea, *sustained by how the realities of capitalist society appear to us in everyday life*, that the current form of organized economic activity is how nature takes its course. This assumption is clearly evident in the idea that both the operation of market forces and attempts to interfere with them produce unintended consequences. Those who most staunchly defend the market believe that attempts by governments to restrict or limit the operation of market forces will almost always produce negative consequences. Challenges to the Keynesian welfare state argue that "wellmeaning" redistributive, tax-supported public policies produced undesirable and even destructive results: high debt, lagging productivity, low growth. Such policies are felt to violate the natural laws governing market activity.

Unintended consequences resulting from the operation of market forces themselves are known as externalities: incidental costs or benefits generated by economic activity that are not taken into account by market prices. Such externalities can be beneficial or harmful, positive or negative. So, for instance, an industry might dump pollutants into a river without measurable cost, but people living downstream from the dumpsite will bear the consequences in contaminated water. On the other hand, a private homeowner may upgrade her yard, but the neighbours may well derive pleasure and perhaps even an increase in their property values. Either way, externalities are held to be the unavoidable by-products of private self-seeking activity.

Whether positive or negative, externalities are viewed by most defenders of the market as forms of misallocation, which can be corrected by state action (holding polluters responsible for the real costs of their activities, for example). There is, of course, considerable contention about the extent of such externalities and how, if at all, they should be compensated for. In effect, this is a debate over the allocative role of the market itself. The more vigorous the free market view, the less likely its proponent will accept that there are many externalities requiring interference (in other words, market failures) and the more likely, its proponent will view the attempt to expand the role of the state in response to externalities as a cover for an assault on private property or market freedoms. Whatever the range of externalities might be, the general assumption is that corrective actions to deal with them, however necessary, are deviations from what should otherwise be the unrestricted operation of market forces.

But the unintended consequences of the market are only unintended on the basis of commitments to commodity production and self-interested maximization. If such commitments are in fact our choice then the consequences generated by acting in a market setting are not just unintended. Rather, they only seem unintended because we do not specifically reflect upon, or deliberate about, the consequences of our productive activity. These consequences are however a social choice, not a fact of nature. Hence, it is possible to speak of *intended unintended consequences.*

By "intended," I do not mean a situation of cause-and-effect, where we willfully and consciously seek to identify means to bring about certain ends. Rather, I mean an inescapable orientation to our social life such that certain things "make sense," while others do not, and so we act in ways that permit us to have some kind of coherent experience from the point of view of our wants, needs and purposes. This idea is central to a philosophical tradition known as phenomenology. A twentieth-century French philosopher identified with phenomenology, Maurice Merleau-Ponty, referring to another philosopher of similar bent, Edmund Husserl, distinguishes between "intentionality of act, which is that of our judgments and of those occasions when we voluntarily take up a position ... and operative intentionality ... or that which produces the natural ... unity of the world and of our life, being apparent in our desires, our evaluations and in the landscape we see, more clearly than in objective knowledge, and furnishing the text which our knowledge tries to translate into precise language. Our relationship to the world, as it is untiringly enunciated within us, is not a thing which can be any further clarified by analysis; philosophy can only place it once more before our eyes and present it for our ratification."[4] The important point for our purposes is that much of what appears to us about ourselves as a fact of nature is rather the product of human activity and understanding: our "operative intentionality" produces the "natural unity" of the world and our relation to this world, not a "thing" that can be presented as a stand alone object. But we don't typically see this: we tend to view ourselves as acted upon under the impact of natural, physical laws, rather than as acting.

The claim advanced here is that externalities just *are* intended unintended consequences, that *market institutions are such that they generate externalities, not necessarily as a result of conscious or deliberate action (and this is why defenders of neo-liberalism and the market are not necessarily propagandists), but nonetheless intentionally, that is, as an embedded commitment in our system of production and exchange*. The interests which organize the production system need the existence of externalities as part of the justification of their power and authority. In one sense, this is because profit-making bodies have an interest in avoiding the full costs of the negative consequences of their activities. But in another, more basic sense, since externalities involve social and not just private costs, their presence can be seen to indicate that significant elements in our social system of production are beyond the capacity of society as a whole to regulate or control. They are seen as if they were natural forces. There can be no "social" economy, only a primarily private one under the direction of private interests.

If this account of the market is plausible, then an economic structure based on commodification and individual maximization does more than shape the material forces at work in society. It also generates a specific conception of who we ultimately are. And this has momentous consequences, for we become beings who acquire the commitment *not* to know certain things about what we are doing.

The case studies in this book and the notion of embedded political theory intended to inform them are ways of trying to bring these matters into focus, to open up the question of reification. I want to conclude by suggesting some implications of the kind of policy analysis attempted here and of thinking in terms of embedded political theory. In particular, I want to indicate how the approach adopted in this book might be of some use in conducting political and social analysis and in considering the tasks of citizenship.

All accounts of our social relations, including our economic relations, are political in the sense that they necessarily deal with our ties to each other and articulate how and to what extent our social bonds realize certain wants, needs and purposes. In illuminating what people do, they unavoidably say something about what people should or should *not* do, or even *be*. In varying degrees, this process of articulation provides a certain kind of evidence of social behaviour that could help us formulate claims and arguments about the nature and structure of society.

The sort of evidence I have in mind here is different from what we might typically think of when we use this term. I mean compelling insight into matters that impinge upon the consciousness and actions of people sharing a common social situation. Such evidence is more than data acquired through empirical methods associated with social scientific practice and organized into research findings that claim to be subject-independent, that is, provide an impartial and objective account of things unsullied by partial, non-scientific considerations. (This is the "objective knowledge" referred to by Merleau-Ponty.) Of course, data collection and presentation have an important role in social inquiry. But the evidence being defended here has to do with the ways in which people come to acquire certain understandings of their world and undertake certain activities. These understandings and activities reflect our capacity to more or less coherently and competently recreate ties which fulfill our purposes and make possible a recognizably human set of social arrangements. Such understandings and activities might best be understood not as facts about us that can be presented, for example, in statistical form, but as modes through which we literally are who we are, with this identity being intertwined with our conceptions of what we are all about. In an ongoing way, these understandings and activities both have (or lack) meaning and value, and can be (and are) interpreted in terms of whether or not they *have* meaning and value. If the data we acquire is to make sense, it must be related to such understandings and activities, and if it makes sense, it already is so related. It doesn't just "stand there," interpreting itself.

Analyses such as those associated with tax policy take for granted this connection between data and the understandings and activities in the context of which this data makes sense.

To claim that people competently and coherently reproduce their social ties and bonds in ways which allow them to make their way within the conditions of their lives is not to claim there are no contradictions or tensions in their consciousness or actions or that there is seamless fit between intentions and outcomes. Indeed, this book has argued that, particularly under the influence of neo-liberal ideas, people do experience such tensions. Yet, at the same time, the presence of contradictions or tensions does not mean that it is impossible to achieve greater clarity in our grasp of society, a clarity that would make more fully possible the realization of our purposes. People always and unavoidably proceed in the course of making sense of self and society to assess states of affairs in light of better or worse, more or less able to fulfill significant purposes, ultimately more or less consistent with important, even essential, human aspirations. In this respect, we necessarily deal with the relation of aspirations to norms, practices and institutions, and how these may realize or thwart, or both realize and thwart, or even thwart by realizing, human wants, needs and purposes. The account in this book of taxation and embedded political theory makes sense only in light of the claim that existing economic relations achieve certain things at the expense of others that may ultimately be more important for us.

In my view, then, there are purposes that are more or less defensible, these do find a place in our culture, and we unavoidably carry them as bases for thinking and acting. Such purposes involve what might be called the boundary conditions of sociability, such that in their disavowal or even absence, we would be dealing with something other than a recognizably human form of life. The analysis of this book is shaped by the claim that the assumptions embedded in contemporary neo-liberal conceptions of appropriate tax policy support purposes that breach these boundary conditions. They do so by denying the possibility of those communal or collective bonds within which such assumptions make sense in the first place. As Charles Lindblom, whose ideas I referred to in Chapter Two, indicated, it is impossible to build an economy, or indeed a society, on the basis that the world is composed exclusively of individual buyers and sellers, self-contained individuals. Communal bonds not only help us make sense of the very neo-liberal assumptions that would deny them, they also make it possible for the self-seeking behaviour these assumptions justify to be contained and rendered compatible with a humane social order.

Obviously this is both a difficult and contestable claim, a matter of normative philosophical speculation and judgment. But far from being a limitation, the presence of philosophical speculation and judgment is a strength. No social science, if it is to be meaningful, can in the end escape them. From the perspective of this understanding of social science, the conceptions of taxation held by the two studies I examined implicitly cast light on how we ought to live together, and they do so necessarily, that is, whether the authors deliberately intended this or not. The very terms that they must use elucidate our situation as humans who share certain ways of being together. In this light, neo-liberal claims misrepresent human possibilities by treating us as if we were natural objects and as if the facts about us were therefore "mere" facts of nature. In so doing, they make it difficult to grasp how these facts are related to our actions and understandings. Neo-liberal claims express a reified or "thing-like" understanding of who we are and are incompatible with a society that would fulfill important wants, needs and purposes.[5]

Yet these claims *do* tell us something about the values and institutions of a market social order. If they are incompatible with important wants, needs and purposes, this is not because they are totally false in the way they describe current social institutions and practices. It is because in important respects they are true. What gives the neo-liberal era its specific character lies in the fact that our institutions and practices have been recast to more strongly emphasize than has been the case for a long time the values of the market and individualism. These have always been part of our culture but not always so powerfully as they are now. As I tried to argue above, when these values get out of hand, they distort social life; they block the fulfillment of other aims. Neo-liberalism makes sense in the measure that society itself fails to achieve important human aspirations, notably the aspirations for community and solidarity. Capitalist societies have in significant respects moved away in recent decades from achieving such aspirations, even though these societies have created the material conditions under which they could do so. In important ways, the issue of taxation expresses this shift. Ideas about taxation illuminate the gap between what a society seems prepared to accept and what it is capable of achieving.

Neo-liberalism claims the mantle of hardheaded realism, while charging its communitarian opponents with a utopian impracticality that requires them to impose their values on a society of individuals defined by their quest for market freedoms. However, the reverse seems more true: the idea that society could be organized to an ever greater extent around the market and its values seems the height of utopianism in the pejorative sense in which neo-liberals typically understand it. And neo-liberals themselves seek to impose their values—witness the suspicion among many who hold rational-choice views about democracy's tendency to encourage politicians to pander for votes, while urging elected representatives to show "courage" and do the "unpopular" by cutting back on government and freeing up the market, whatever voters might want or think they want.

Whatever one's normative commitments, it is impossible to escape the bonds of collective life. These bonds are not impediments to individual fulfillment but facilitators. In asking the question "who am I?" we cannot avoid the question "who are we?"

In 1987, British Prime Minister, Margaret Thatcher, an influential exponent of neo-liberal views, was widely quoted as proclaiming: "There is no such thing as society."[6] She was wrong. To be sure, this is a value judgment. But in my view it is also the insight of a social science truly attuned to the complexity of human beings, their goals and purposes, and the need for people to find a humane way to live together. I hope this book has at least made this claim plausible and what it ultimately contends: that in describing what we think society *is*, we cannot avoid saying what it should be.

Notes

1. *The Globe and Mail* (Toronto), July 24, 2002, B1, B6.
2. The origin of the term is generally attributed to the twentieth-century Hungarian Marxist philosopher, Georg Lukacs. See his *History and Class Consciousness: Studies in Marxist Dialectics* (1923), trans. by Rodney Livingstone (London: Merlin Press, 1971). For a sobering and insightful, if demanding, account of reification from the perspective of viewing humans as things, see Theodor W. Adorno, "Education After Auschwitz" (1967), in T.W. Adorno, *Critical Models: Interventions and Catchwords*, trans. with a preface by Henry W. Pickford (New York: Columbia University Press, 1998), 191–204.
3. For different but complementary accounts of the phenomenon of reification, even if the term itself is not used, see, for example, Roberto Mangabeira Unger, *False Necessity: Anti-Necessitarian Social Theory in the Service of Radical Democracy* (Cambridge: Cambridge University Press, 1987); Fred L. Block, *Postindustrial Possibilities: A Critique of Economic Discourse* (Berkeley: University of California Press, 1990); and Linda McQuaig, *The Cult of Impotence: Selling the Myth of Powerlessness in the Global Economy* (Toronto: Viking, 1998). From the point of view of theorists of reification, neo-liberalism is not the only culprit. Lukacs, for one, felt it to be a pervasive quality throughout capitalist society. During the era of the Keynesian welfare state, the then dominant ideas tended in many instances to express reification; hence the period is sometimes viewed as being one of "technocratic Keynesianism."
4. Maurice Merleau-Ponty, *Phenomenology of Perception*, trans. by Colin Smith (London and Henley: Routledge & Kegan Paul, 1962), xviii.
5. For a similar argument, see Dryzek, *Democracy in Capitalist Times*, ch.5. Even tax cutting governments of a neo-liberal stripe may be starting to come to this view. Recently, both Ontario, an especially vigorous practitioner of tax cuts, and Newfoundland have announced delays in implementing proposed reductions, while in its current budget Alberta has increased existing taxes (although not the personal income tax) and reduced the size of an earlier announced reduction in corporate income taxes. *The Globe and Mail* (Toronto), June 18, 2002, A1, A5; June 19, 2002, A8. They may have come to the conclusion that the range of socially necessary tasks for government to carry out exceeds what the neo-liberal position claims.
6. Ibid., 119.

Bibliography

Ackerly, Brooke A. 2000. *Political Theory and Feminist Social Criticism*. Cambridge: Cambridge University Press.
Adorno, Theodor W. 1998. *Critical Models: Interventions and Catchwords*, trans. with a preface by Henry W. Pickford. New York: Columbia University Press.
Asper, Israel H. 1970. *The Benson Iceberg: A Critical Analysis of the White Paper on Tax Reform in Canada*. Toronto: Clarke, Irwin and Co.
Bale, Gordon. 1988. "The Carter Report: Good Ideas Remain Good Ideas." In W. Neil Brooks, ed., *The Quest for Tax Reform: The Royal Commission on Taxation Twenty Years Later*. Toronto: Carswell.
Beck, Ulrich. 1999. *World Risk Society*. Cambridge: Polity Press.
Benhabib, Seyla, ed. 1996. *Democracy and Difference: Contesting the Boundaries of the Political*. Princeton: Princeton University Press.
Blackburn, Robin. 2002. "The Enron Debacle and the Pension Crisis." *New Left Review* 14 (March-April), 26–51.
Bohman, James, and William Rehg, eds. 1997. *Deliberative Democracy*. Cambridge, MA: The MIT Press.
Bradford, Neil. 1999. "The Policy Influence of Economic Ideas: Interests, Institutions and Innovations in Canada." *Studies in Political Economy* 59 (Summer) 17–60.
Brooks, Neil. 1998. "Flattening the Claims of the Flat Taxers." *The Dalhousie Law Journal* 21, 2 (Fall).
Brown, Lorne A., Joseph K. Roberts and John W. Warnock. 1999. *Saskatchewan Politics from Left to Right '44–'99*. Regina: Hinterland Publications.
Brown, Robert D. 1999. "Tax Reform and Tax Reduction: Let's Do the Job Right." *Canadian Tax Journal* 47, 2. 1999., 182-205.
Brownstone, M. 1971. "The Douglas-Lloyd Governments: Innovation and Bureaucratic Adaptation." In Laurier LaPierre et al., eds., *Essays on the Left: Essays in Honour of T. C. Douglas*. Toronto/Montreal: McClelland and Stewart Limited.
Buchanan, James M. 1991. "Politics Without Romance: A Sketch of Positive Public Choice and Its Normative Implications." In Alan Hamlin and Philip Petit, eds., *Contemporary Political Theory*. New York: Macmillan.
Burstyn, Varda, ed. 1985. *Women, Class, Family and the State*. Toronto: Garamond Press.
———. 1990. *Rites of Men: Manhood, Politics, and the Culture of Sport*. Toronto: University of Toronto Press.
Campbell, Murray. 2000. "Have compassionate Canadians gone greedy?" *The Globe and Mail*, May 6. Toronto.
Campbell, Robert M. 1999. "The Fourth Fiscal Era: Can There Be a 'Post Neoconservative' Fiscal Policy." In Leslie Pal, ed., *How Ottawa Spends 1999–2000: Shape Shifting Canadian Governance Toward the 21st Century*. Toronto: Oxford University Press.

Canada, Agriculture and Agri-Food Canada. 2002. *Farm Income, Financial Conditions and Government Assistance Data Book.* March.

Canada. 1967. *Report of the Royal Commission on Taxation* 5 Vols. Ottawa: Queen's Printer.

———. 1985. *Report of the Royal Commission on The Economic Union and Development Prospects for Canada,* 3 vols. Ottawa: Minister of Supply and Services.

Canada, Statistics Canada. *The Daily.* Various issues.

Chomsky, Noam. 1989. *Necessary Illusions: Thought Control in Democratic Societies.* Toronto: CBC Enterprises.

Chorney, Harold, and Phillip Hansen. 1985. "Neo-conservatism, Social Democracy and 'Province Building':The Experience of Manitoba." *Canadian Review of Sociology and Anthropology* 22, 1 (February), 1–29.

Chorney, Harold. 1988. *Sound Finance and Other Delusions: Deficit & Debt Management in the Age of Neo-Liberal Economics.* Working Paper No.4, Department of Political Science, Concordia University, Ottawa. March.

———. 1989. *The Deficit and Debt Management: An Alternative to Monetarism.* Ottawa: Canadian Centre for Policy Alternatives. April.

Clarkson, Stephen. 2002. *Uncle Sam and Us: Globalization, Neoconservatism, and the Canadian State.* Toronto and Washington, DC: University of Toronto Press and Woodrow Wilson Center Press.

Clement, Wallace, and John Myles. 1994. *Relations of Ruling: Class and Gender in Postindustrial Societies.* Montreal and Kingston: McGill-Queen's University Press.

Cohen, Jean L. 1982. *Class and Civil Society: The Limits of Marxian Critical Theory.* Amherst, MA: University of Massachusetts Press.

Cohen, Jean L. and Andrew Arato. 1992. *Civil Society and Political Theory.* Cambridge, MA, and London: The MIT Press.

Cohen, Joshua, and Joel Rogers. 1983. *On Democracy: Toward a Transformation of American Society.* New York: Penguin Books.

Coleman, Frank M. 1977. *Hobbes and America: Exploring the Constitutional Foundations.* Toronto and Buffalo: University of Toronto Press.

Cunningham, Frank. 2002. *Democratic Theory: A Critical Introduction.* London and New York: Routledge.

"The cuts kick in next year." 2000. *The Leader-Post.* Regina, December 30.

Dawson, Lance. 1996. *Evolution of Social Housing Policy in Saskatchewan: A Comparative Study of Regina and Moose Jaw, 1944–1982.* Unpublished M.A. Thesis, Department of History, University of Regina.

DeLue, Steven M. 2002. *Political Thinking, Political Theory, and Civil Society.* Second edition. New York: Longman.

Desai, Maghnad. 2002. *Marx's Revenge: The Resurgence of Capitalism and the Death of Statist Socialism.* London and New York: Verso.

Descombes, Vincent. 1994. "Is there an objective spirit?" In James Tully, ed., *Philosophy in an Age of Pluralism: The philosophy of Charles in question.* Cambridge: Cambridge University Press.

Dryzek, John S. 1996. *Democracy in Capitalist Times: Ideals, Limits, and Struggles.* Oxford: Oxford University Press.

———. 2000. *Deliberative Democracy and Beyond: Liberals, Critics, Contestations.* Oxford: Oxford University Press.

Dunn, Christopher, and David Laycock. 1992. "Saskatchewan: Innovation and Competition in the Agricultural Heartland." In Keith Brownsey and Michael Howlett, eds., *The Provincial State: Politics in Canada's Provinces and Territories*. Mississauga, ON: Copp Clark Pitman.
Dyck, Rand. 2000. *Canadian Politics: Critical Approaches*. Third edition. Scarborough, ON: Nelson.
Eager, Evelyn. 1980. *Saskatchewan Government: Politics and Pragmatism*. Saskatoon: Western Producer Books.
Eaton, Kenneth. 1966. *Essays in Taxation*. Toronto: Canadian Tax Foundation.
Edelman, Murray. 1977. *Political Language: Words That Succeed and Policies That Fail*. New York: Academic Press.
———. 2001. *The Politics of Misinformation*. Cambridge: Cambridge University Press.
Eisler, Dale A. 1987. *Rumours of Glory: Saskatchewan and the Thatcher Years*. Edmonton: Hurtig.
Elliott, Anthony. 1999. "Introduction." In Anthony Elliott, ed., *The Blackwell Reader in Contemporary Social Theory*. Oxford: Blackwell Publishers.
Engels, Friedrich. 1892. *Socialism: Utopian and Scientific* (originally published 1878; English edition 1892). In Robert C. Tucker *The Marx-Engels Reader* Second Edition. New York: W.W. Norton & Company.
Ernst, Alan. 1992. "From Liberal Constitutionalism to Neoconservatism: North American Free Trade and the Politics of the C. D. Howe Institute." *Studies in Political Economy* 39 (Autumn), 109–40.
Ferber, Marianne A., and Julie A. Nelson, eds. 1993. *Beyond Economic Man: Feminist Theory and Economics*. Chicago and London: University of Chicago Press.
Finkel, Alvin. 1997. *Our Lives: Canada after 1945*. Toronto: James Lorimer & Company Ltd.
Fraser, Nancy. 1997. *Justice Interruptus: Critical Reflections on the "Postsocialist" Condition*. New York & London: Routledge.
———. 1998. "Heterosexism, Misrecognition, and Capitalism: A Response to Judith Butler." *New Left Review* 1/228 (March-April), 140–9.
———. 2000. "Rethinking Recognition." *New Left Review* 3 (May-June), 107–21.
Frisby, David, and Derek Sayer. 1986. *Society*. London and New York: Tavistock.
Gardner, Robert. 1081. "Tax Reform and Class Interests: The Fate of Progressive Reform, 1967–1972." *Canadian Taxation* 3, 4 (Winter), 245–57.
Giddens, Anthony. 1994. *Beyond Left and Right: The Future of Radical Politics*. Stanford, CA: Stanford University Press.
Gillespie, W. Irwin. 1990. *Tax, Borrow and Spend: Financing Federal Spending in Canada, 1867-1990*. Ottawa: Carleton University Press.
Gitlin, Todd. 1980. *The Whole World's Watching: Mass Media in the Making and Unmaking of the New Left*. Berkeley: University of California Press.
Gould, Carol. 1980. *Marx's Social Ontology: Individuality and Community in Marx's Theory of Social Reality*. Cambridge, MA, & London, England: The MIT Press.
Grabb, Edward G. 1997. *Theories of Social Inequality: Classical and Contemporary Perspectives*. Third edition. Toronto: Harcourt Brace & Company.
Gruneau, Richard, and David Whitson. 1993. *Hockey Night in Canada: Sports, Identities and Cultural Politics*. Toronto: Garamond Press.
Guest, Dennis. 1997. *The Emergence of Social Security in Canada*. Third edition.

Vancouver: University of British Columbia Press.

Gullickson, David P.M. 1990. *Uranium Mining, the State, and Public Policy in Saskatchewan, 1971–1982: The Limits of the Social Democratic Imagination*. Unpublished M.A. Thesis, Department of Sociology and Social Studies, University of Regina.

Hale, Geoffrey. 2000. "The Tax on Income and the Growing Decentralization of Canada's Personal Income Tax System." In Harvey Lazar, ed., *Canada: The State of the Federation 1999/2000*. Montreal and Kingston: McGill-Queen's University Press.

———. 2002. *The Politics of Taxation in Canada*. Peterborough: Broadview Press.

Hall, Peter A., ed. 1989. *The Political Power of Economic Ideas: Keynesianism Across Nations*. Princeton, NJ: Princeton University Press.

Hansen, Phillip. 1994. "Saskatchewan: The Failure of Political Imagination." *Studies in Political Economy* 43 (Spring), 161–7.

Hartsock, Nancy C.M. 1985. *Sex and Power: Toward a Feminist Historical Materialism*. Boston: Northeastern University Press.

Hegel, G.W.F. 1991. *Elements of the Philosophy of Right*. 1820. Ed. by Allen W. Wood, trans. by H.B. Nisbet. Cambridge: Cambridge University Press.

Held, David, and Anthony McGrew, eds. 2000. *The Global Transformations Reader: An Introduction to the Globalization Debate*. Cambridge: Polity Press.

Held, David. 1996. *Models of Democracy* Second edition. Cambridge: Polity Press.

Held, David, et al. 1999. *Global Transformations: Politics, Economics and Culture*. Cambridge: Polity Press.

Hobbes, Thomas. 1988. *Leviathan*. 1651. Ed. by C.B. Macpherson. London: Penguin Books.

Holmstrom, Nancy. 2000. "Rationality, Solidarity, and Public Goods." In Anatole Anton, Milton Fisk and Nancy Holmstrom, eds., *Not For Sale: In Defense of Public Goods*. Boulder, CO: Westview Press.

Horowitz, Asher and Gad Horowitz. 1988. *"Everywhere They Are in Chains" Political Theory from Rousseau to Marx*. Scarborough, ON: Nelson.

Howlett, Michael, Alex Netherton and M. Ramesh. 1999. *The Political Economy of Canada: An Introduction*. Second edition. Oxford and New York: Oxford University Press.

Jackson, Andrew. 2001. "Can There Be a 'Second Wave' in the Third Millennium?" *Studies in Political Economy* 65 (Summer).

Jessop, Bob. 1993. "Towards a Schumpeterian Workfare State? Preliminary Remarks on Post-Fordist Political Economy." *Studies in Political Economy* 40 (Spring), 7–39.

Keane, John. 1993. "Stretching the Limits of the Democratic Imagination." In Joseph H. Carens, ed., *Democracy and Possessive Individualism: The Intellectual Legacy of C. B. Macpherson*. Albany, NY: State University of New York Press.

———. 2002. "Whatever Happened to Democracy?" A public lecture delivered for the Institute for Public Policy Research, London, 27 March. Available at HtmlResAnchor www.wmin.ac.uk/esd/JKWhateverHappenedtoDemocracy.htm.

Knuttila, Murray, and Wendee Kubik. 2000. *State Theories: Classical, Global and Feminist Perspectives*. Third edition. Halifax & London: Fernwood Publishing/Zed Books.

Kuttner, Robert. 1999. *Everything for Sale: The Virtues and Limits of Markets*.

Chicago: University of Chicago Press.
Kymlicka, Will. 2002. *Contemporary Political Philosophy: An Introduction*. Second edition. Toronto: Oxford University Press.
Lasch, Christopher. 1978. *The Culture of Narcissism: American Life in an Age of Diminishing Expectations*. New York: W.W. Norton & Company.
Law Commission of Canada. 2002. *Renewing Democracy: Debating Electoral Reform in Canada*. Canada: Law Commission of Canada.
Leibritz, W., et al. 1999. "Taxation and Economic Performance." OECD Working Papers, No.176.
Levine, Andrew. 2002. *Engaging Political Philosophy: from Hobbes to Rawls*. Malden, MA: Blackwell Publishers.
Lindblom, Charles E. 1977. *Politics and Markets: The World's Political-Economic Systems*. New York: Basic Books.
Little, Bruce. 2002. "Social spending now following a new pattern." *The Globe and Mail*. Toronto, November 18.
Lloyd, W.S. 1962. "The Positive Role of Government." *Canadian Public Administration* December, 404–5. Cited in M. Brownstone, 1971, "The Douglas-Lloyd Governments: Innovation and Bureaucratic Adaptation," in Laurier LaPierre, et al., eds., *Essays on the Left: Essays in Honour of T.C. Douglas*. Toronto/Montreal: McClelland and Stewart.
Lukacs, Georg. 1971. *History and Class Consciousness: Studies in Marxist Dialectics*. 1923. Trans. by Rodney Livingstone. London: Merlin Press.
MacEwan, Arthur. 1999. *Neo-Liberalism or Democracy? Economic Strategy, Markets, and Alternative for the 21st Century*. Halifax: Fernwood Publishing.
Macpherson, C.B. 1962. *The Political Theory of Possessive Individualism: Hobbes to Locke*. Oxford: Oxford University Press.
———. 1973. *Democratic Theory: Essays in Retrieval*. Oxford: Clarendon Press.
———. 1976. "Humanist Democracy and Elusive Marxism: A Response to Minogue and Svacek." *Canadian Journal of Political Science* IX:3 (September), 423–30.
———. 1977. *The Life and Times of Liberal Democracy*. Oxford: Oxford University Press.
———. 1985. *The Rise and Fall of Economic Justice and Other Essays*. Oxford and New York: Oxford University Press.
Marx, Karl, and Friedrich Engels. 1992. *The Communist Manifesto*. Originally written 1848; this edition 1888. New York and Toronto: Bantam Books.
———. 2000. *The German Ideology* (1846). In David McLellan (ed.), *Karl Marx: Selected Writings* Second Edition. Oxford: Oxford University Press.
Mayhew, Anne. 2001. "Human Agency, Cumulative Causation, and the State." *Journal of Economic Issues* XXV, 2 (June), 239–50.
McBride, Stephen, and John Shields. 1997. *Dismantling a Nation: The Transition to Corporate Rule in Canada*. Second edition. Halifax: Fernwood Publishing.
McChesney, Robert W. 1999. *Rich Media, Poor Democracy: Communication Politics in Dubious Times*. Urbana and Chicago: University of Illinois Press.
McLean, Scott, David A. Schultz and Manfred B. Steger. 2002. *Social Capital: Critical Perspectives on Community and "Bowling Alone."* New York and London: New York University Press.
McLellan, David, ed. 2000. *Karl Marx: Selected Writings*. Second edition. Oxford: Oxford University Press.
McQuaig, Linda. 1987. *Behind Closed Doors: How the Rich Won Control of*

Canada's Tax System and Ended Up Richer. Toronto: Viking/Penguin.

Merleau-Ponty, Maurice. 1962. *Phenomenology of Perception*. Trans. by Colin Smith. London and Henley: Routledge & Kegan Paul.

Moe, Andrea. 2001. "Elusive Neutrality: The Recent Debate Surrounding the Child Care Expense Deduction and Income Splitting in Canada." Paper presented to the Annual Meeting, Canadian Political Science Association, Laval University, Quebec City, May.

"More work – less cash." 2001. *The Leader-Post*. Regina., August 11.

"Sask. real wages drop seven per cent since 1992." 2002. *The Leader-Post*. Regina., October 21.

Mouffe, Chantel, ed. 1992. *Dimensions of Radical Democracy: Pluralism, Citizenship, Community*. London: Verso.

Mueller, Denies C. 1979. *Public Choice*. Cambridge: Cambridge University Press.

Nozick, Robert. 1974. *Anarchy, State and Utopia*. New York: Basic Books.

Offe, Claus. 1994. "Interdependence, Difference and Limited State Capacity." In Glen Drover and Patrick Kerans, eds., *New Approaches to Welfare Theory*. Aldershot, England: Edward Elgar.

———. 1996. *Modernity and the State: East, West*. Cambridge, MA: The MIT Press.

Olsen, Greg M. 2002. *The Politics of the Welfare State: Canada, Sweden, and the United States*. Don Mills, ON: Oxford University Press.

Panitch, Leo. 1993. "Beyond the Crisis of the Tax State? From Fair Taxation to Structural Reform." In Allan M. Maslove, ed., *Fairness in Taxation: Exploring the Principles*. Toronto: University of Toronto Press.

———. 1995. "Elites, Classes, and Power in Canada." In Michael S. Whittington and Glen Williams, eds., *Canadian Politics in the 1990s*. Fourth edition. Scarborough, ON: Nelson.

Parkin, Frank. 1979. *Marxism and Class Theory: A Bourgeois Critique*. New York: Columbia University Press.

Pateman, Carole. 1975. "Sublimation and Reification: Locke, Wolin and the Liberal Democratic Conception of the Political." *Politics and Society* 15, 441–67.

Perry, David B. 1997. *Financing the Canadian Federation, 1867 to 1995: Setting the Stage for Change*. Toronto: Canadian Tax Foundation.

Philipps, Lisa. 2001. "Women, Taxes and Social Programs." Paper presented at "Breakfast on the Hill" Seminar, Humanities and Social Sciences Federation of Canada, Ottawa, ON, April 26.

Phillips, Anne. 1993. *Democracy and Difference*. University Park, PA: The Pennsylvania State University Press.

Pierson, Christopher. 1998. *Beyond the Welfare State: The New Political Economy of Welfare*. Second edition. University Park, PA: Pennsylvania State University Press.

Pitkin, Hannah Fenichel. 1993. *Wittgenstein and Justice*. 1972. Berkeley: University of California Press.

Pitsula, James and Ken Rasmussen. 1990. *Privatizing a Province: The New Right in Saskatchewan*. Vancouver: New Star Books.

Polanyi, Karl. 1957. *The Great Transformation*. 1944. Boston: Beacon Press.

Province of Saskatchewan. 1965. *Report of the Royal Commission on Taxation*. Regina: Queen's Printer.

———. 1988. *A Dialogue on Saskatchewan Tax Reform*. Regina: Department of Finance.

———. 2001. Agriculture and Food *Agricultural Statistics 2000*. December.
———. 2001. *Budget Address*. March 30.
Province of Saskatchewan. Bureau of Statistics. 2001. *Economic Review 2001*, Number Fifty Five. December.
———. Bureau of Statistics. 2002. *Saskatchewan Provincial Economic Accounts 2001*. May.
Putnam, Robert. 2000. *Bowling Alone: The Collapse and Revival of American Community*. New York: Simon and Schuster.
Rasmussen, Ken. 2001. "Saskatchewan: From Entrepreneurial State to Embedded State." In Keith Brownsey and Michael Howlett, eds., *The Provincial State in Canada: Politics in the Provinces and Territories*. Peterborough, ON: Broadview Press.
Rawls, John. 1999. *A Theory of Justice* Revised edition. Cambridge, MA: The Belknap Press of Harvard University Press.
Richards, John, and Larry Pratt. 1979. *Prairie Capitalism: Power and Influence in the New West*. Toronto: McClelland and Stewart.
Robinson, Ian. 1993. "The NAFTA, Democracy and Continental Economic Integration: Trade Policy as if Democracy Mattered." In Susan D. Phillips, ed., *How Ottawa Spends 1993–1994: A More Democratic Canada…?* Ottawa: Carleton University Press.
Rosenof, Theodore. 1997. *Economics in the Long Run: New Deal Theorists and their Legacies, 1933–1993*. Chapel Hill and London: University of North Carolina Press.
Rousseau, Jean-Jacques. 1993. *The Social Contract and Discourses*. Trans. and introduced by G.D.H. Cole; rev. and augmented by J.H. Brumfit and John C. Hall; updated by P.D. Jimack. London: J.M. Dent.
Rushton, Michael. 1999. "Tax Policy and Income Support: An Analysis of Effective Marginal Tax Rates and Saskatchewan Families." Paper presented to Saskatchewan Personal Income Tax Review Committee, June 17. .
———. 2000. "Interprovincial Tax Competition and Tax Reform in Saskatchewan." *Canadian Tax Journal* 48, 2, 374–88.
Saskatchewan Personal Income Tax Review Committee. 1999. *Final Report and Recommendations*. Regina: Government of Saskatchewan.
Schumpeter, Joseph. 1975. *Capitalism, Socialism, and Democracy* Third edition. 1950. New York: Harper Colophon Books.
———. 1991. "The Crisis of the Tax State." 1918. In Richard Swedberg, ed., *Joseph A. Schumpeter: The Economics and Sociology of Capitalism*. Princeton: Princeton University Press.
Scitovsky, Tibor. 1976. *The Joyless Economy: An Inquiry into Human Satisfaction and Consumer Dissatisfaction*. Oxford: Oxford University Press.
Shields, John, and B. Mitchell Evans. 1998. *Shrinking the State: Globalization and Public Service "Reform."* Halifax: Fernwood Publishing.
Silver, Jim. 1996. *Thin Ice: Money, Politics and the Demise of an NHL Franchise*. Halifax: Fernwood Publishing.
Simon, Henry. 1965. *Personal Taxation: The Definition of Income as a Problem of Fiscal Policy*. 1938. Chicago and London: University of Chicago Press.
Smith, David. 1975. *Prairie Liberalism: The Liberal Party in Saskatchewan 1905-71*. Toronto and Buffalo: University of Toronto Press.
Stirling, Bob. 2001. "Transitions in Rural Saskatchewan." In Howard A. Leeson, ed.,

Saskatchewan Politics: Into the Twenty-First Century. Regina: Canadian Plains Research Centre.

Taylor, Charles. 1979. *Hegel and Modern Society*. Cambridge: Cambridge University Press.

———. 1985. *Philosophy and the Human Sciences: Philosophical Papers 2*. Cambridge: Cambridge University Press.

———. 1989. "Cross-Purposes: The Liberal-Communitarian Debate." In Nancy Rosenblum, ed., *Liberalism and the Moral Life*. Cambridge, MA: Harvard University Press.

———. 1995. *Philosophical Arguments*. Cambridge, MA: Harvard University Press.

"Tax cuts kick in next year." 2000. *The Leader-Post* (Regina), December 30.

"Thatcher states taxation report not gov't policy." 1965 *The Leader-Post* (Regina), July 8.

Tucker, Robert C. 1978. *The Marx-Engels Reader*. Second edition. New York: W.W. Norton & Company.

von Hayek, Friedrich A. 1960. *The Constitution of Liberty*. Chicago: University of Chicago Press.

von Mises, Ludwig. 1949. *Human Action: A Treatise on Economics*. New Haven: Yale University Press.

Vosko, Leah. 2002. "The Pasts and Futures of Feminist Political Economy in Canada: Reviving the Debate." *Studies in Political Economy* 68 (Summer), 55–83.

Westphal, Kenneth. 1993. "The basic context and structure of Hegel's *Philosophy of Right*." In Frederick C. Beiser, ed., *The Cambridge Companion to Hegel*. Cambridge: Cambridge University Press.

Workman, Thom. 1996. B*anking on Deception: The Discourse of Fiscal Crisis*. Halifax: Fernwood Publishing.

———. 1999. "Hegemonic Modulation and the Discourse of Fiscal Crisis." *Studies in Political Economy* 59 (Summer), 61–89.

Young, Iris Marion. 2001 "Activist Challenges to Deliberative Democracy." *Political Theory*. 29,5 (October), 670–90.